Testimonials

In this nifty and fabulous volume, Ed Barks gives the corporate communicator tons of good advice on how to get that important "seat at the table" and how to use it when there. Helpful to the communicator as it is, I hope every reader will forward a clandestine copy to the CEO, the one who needs to understand the all-important role that strategic communications plays in managing a business or organization, (and how to manage relations with government officials, an increasingly vital element of external relations for any senior executive).

Mike McCurry was White House Press Secretary to President Bill Clinton and is of counsel to Public Strategies Washington, Inc.

How we consume, produce and yes, even influence news continues to change rapidly. As a leader in his field, Ed Barks has studied new methods of communication and brought C-Suite communicators a present day playbook on how to help top executives thrive in an ever-changing information landscape.

Betsy Fischer Martin, Former Executive Producer of "Meet the Press" and Principal, Fischer Martin Media

Ed Barks' latest book is full of winning strategies to help communicators — whether they partner with key leaders on the inside, or provide outside counsel as consultants — build trust and offer solid advice to executives. Ed provides a common sense manual for today's communicator. This wisdom will surely light the path for tomorrow's influencers.

Anthony Shop, Co-Founder & Chief Strategy Officer of Social Driver, and Chairman of the National Digital Roundtable

A+ STRATEGIES FOR C-SUITE COMMUNICATIONS

Turning Today's Leaders into Tomorrow's Influencers

ED BARKS

Published by:
Ogmios Publishing
Berryville, Virginia

Paperback ISBN 13: 978-0-9742538-7-9
Ebook ISBN 13: 978-0-9742538-6-2

This publication is designed to provide accurate and authoritative information in regard to the subject matter covered. It is sold with the understanding that the publisher is not engaged in rendering legal, accounting, or other professional service. If legal advice or other expert assistance is required, the services of a competent professional person should be sought.
    – From a Declaration of Principles jointly adopted by a committee of the American Bar Association and a Committee of Publishers and Associations

Discounts for bulk purchases are available for corporate and association meetings, professional societies, and book clubs. Call (540) 955-0600 to make arrangements.

Ed Barks is available to speak at your next annual meeting, conference, or retreat. To learn more, visit www.barkscomm.com/speaker or call (540) 955-0600.

Ed likes to hear from his readers. Email him at ebarks@barkscomm.com. Visit him online at www.barkscomm.com.

Library of Congress Cataloging-in-publication Data
Barks, Ed
A+ Strategies for C-Suite Communications: Turning Today's Leaders into Tomorrow's Influencers
Includes index
Categories:
Business & Money: Management & Leadership: Strategy & Competition
Business & Money: Marketing & Sales: Public Relations
Politics & Social Sciences: Politics & Government: Public Affairs & Policy: Communication Policy
Library of Congress Control Number: 2018964491

Ebook version Aaron

Dedications

To Celeste and Polly, the absolute lights of my life.

And to Oliver Woshinsky. Wise professor. Fast friend. Inspiration for how a life should be lived. With deepest gratitude for helping me land in Washington, D.C., all those years ago.

Contents

PREFACE

The classic comic Rodney Dangerfield constantly complained, "I don't get no respect." Communications and government relations experts can relate.

When a financial issue arises in your company, the accountants and auditors get the call. In the health care realm, the physicians and scientists hold sway when a new therapy goes to market. At the first sign of a hack attack, the IT staff is summoned.

Yet there is a common element to all these situations: The need to state your case to influence the public. Where are the expert strategic communicators? Often shut out.

I've heard from many communicators over the years who are frustrated by this lack of attention. Sure, sometimes it's an ego thing. But the good ones realize their businesses suffer when poor messaging and delivery manifest. The company's reputation declines. Its stock price dips. Their own career prospects deteriorate.

I tried to figure out how I could best help. The solution? You're looking at it.

I dug deep into the notion of how communications and government relations experts can best influence their C-suite leadership. The fact is there is not much of a comprehensive nature to be found. Most of the sources I found (and most of the recommended reading lists contained in those volumes) were from the 1990s or earlier. The classics are all well and good, but much has changed in the ways we communicate. Thus, the need for this professional resource.

This is not to say that the advice from experts in finance, marketing, and IT is always heeded. They, too, experience similar frustrations. Yet out of this negativity comes opportunity. If you merge forces with colleagues in those areas, you stand to increase your odds of persuading the top brass. Moreover, if you guide them toward becoming more effective communicators, you are likely to create some strong allies.

My aim in writing this book is practical (I tend to be a pretty pragmatic guy, not much of one for navel gazing or, heaven forbid, "motivational" exhortations). *A+ Strategies for C-Suite Communications: Turning Today's Leaders into Tomorrow's Influencers* is a hands-on guide for senior executives seeking to

i

persuade their C-suite about the value of an organized, long-range, strategic communications program. It is not intended to be used as a textbook, though university instructors may find it useful.

Who stands to benefit? Broadly speaking, it is those professionals who prepare or deliver messages for external audiences and those who hire consultants to do that work.

The prime beneficiaries are those senior communications and public affairs pros who directly counsel their C-suite. Their domains encompass areas like media relations; federal, state, and local government affairs; investor relations; and public relations.

If you already inhabit the C-suite, there's plenty here for you. The strategy, insights, and techniques are, ultimately, intended for you – to help with your day-to-day responsibilities; to make your business more profitable and your career more robust in the long run; and to help you earn clout in your company, your industry, and beyond.

Vice presidents, directors, and managers in a bevy of disciplines also benefit from enhanced communications skills. Regardless of your background – be it accounting, marketing, personnel issues, or any number of other areas – there is plenty here for you that can help pave a smoother career path.

Junior practitioners will also find the book useful. Although they may not have a direct relationship with their C-suite officers, good ideas they put forth can percolate their way up the chain of command. Plus, as their careers mature, they may find themselves climbing into more senior positions that do feature that direct relationship.

Here's one thing you won't find. Books today seem to thrive on stories at the expense of the practical strategic advice that communications and public affairs experts crave. While you'll find plenty of stories and personal anecdotes in these pages, my ultimate goal is to empower you with strategies you can use.

Some personal notes: My everlasting love and gratitude to my wife, Celeste, who has been a constant source of encouragement and support over our 30-plus years of marriage. And my deepest love and thanks to my daughter, Polly, who contributed her talents to this work and who has always remained close, whether living nearby or overseas.

Thanks, too, to the many individuals who have guided me through the years during my career in communications and in radio broadcasting. In particular, my gratitude goes out to those many colleagues I have met through involvements in the National Press Club, American Society of Association Executives, Institute of Management Consultants, and Association for Talent Development.

Where would I be without my beta reading team – those dedicated and unselfish experts who reviewed the manuscript and offered sage comments. You made this a much more valuable resource. A huge thank you to Timothy S. Brown, Patricia E. Garrett, Lorien Reynolds, and Malini Wilkes. You have no idea how much guidance and inspiration you provided, stopping me from running off the rails in some cases. It goes without saying that any remaining errors are mine and mine alone.

And a big round of thanks to Robin Sullivan and Michael J. Sullivan, my book sherpas. Your wisdom, generosity, and encouragement have been essential to making this volume a reality.

Kudos and thanks to Brian Sansoni, Vice President, Communication & Outreach, American Cleaning Institute, for coming up with the book's title. I asked around for suggestions, then crowdsourced some of the choices. Brian's submission polled quite well, so *A+ Strategies for C-Suite Communications* is born.

What a joy it was to reconnect with Sheryl Bauerschmidt, who served as copy editor. She remains a pro's pro and a delight to work with.

And to you, dear reader: Your sustained professional development is by no means static, so I hope you will think of this book you hold in your hands as an evolving work. That means your ideas and suggestions are more than welcome. I like to hear from my readers and I'm always in learning mode, so visit my web site at www.barkscomm.com. Then send me an email and let's get the discussion going.

INTRODUCTION

Communications strategy and sustained professional development. Those are the central tenets of this book.

Why the concentration on those issues? Communications strategy is sorely lacking in too many businesses. When an issue arises, the knee-jerk reaction is to turn to tactics. You've probably heard ideas like these:

"Let's issue a news release."

"Maybe we should pitch our CEO for that keynote at our association's annual meeting."

"The government relations team needs to see the chairman of the Senate committee right away."

These notions are pure tactics with no forethought of a larger goal. It's as if you try to solve the immediate problem of a leaky roof by placing a bucket under the drip, ignoring the strategic need to repair the shingles.

Tactics are a necessary component of any meaningful campaign, don't get me wrong. But your tactics need to flow from your strategy, and too many companies shun that step.

As for the focus on sustained professional development, this has long been a pet peeve of mine. To use an example, I've led many a media training session over my more than 20 years in business. My everlasting frustration is the view that someone like me can work with a C-suite executive once and they're cured. Like magic, over the course of a few hours they understand everything they need to know about dealing with the media, speaking in public, or advocating before policymakers. I can only dream that I'm that good.

No, it doesn't work like that. Gaining influence in any area means continuous, diligent, nose-to-the-grindstone work over time. Smart executives understand this. Yet even they often ignore the resources – both internal and external – they have at their disposal. With the crush of everyday business, sharpening their communications edge gets left by the wayside. The following chapters are meant to pave a smooth road from leader to influencer.

Chapter One shines the light on communications strategy, that frequently lacking piece of the puzzle. It discusses the all-important need for communications and government relations executives to speak truth to their C-suite leaders, even suggesting ways to gain that seat at the decision-making table and to capture credit for their contributions. It also includes ideas for raising your CEO's influencer profile; do you think that might gain you some bonus points? The bottom line lesson: Always put strategy before tactics.

The coverage of communications strategy continues in Chapter Two, highlighting how to put together that strategy and some of the benefits gained from implementing it. The chapter includes a case study with recommendations on how to get C-suite buy-in for your plans.

Media relations is the focus of Chapter Three. To be sure, there are suggestions for enhancing your company's media outreach capabilities. The chapter goes beyond those tactics to explain why reporters act like they do and how you can place your C-suite influencers on an equal footing. Also included are some guidelines to ensure that your future media training programs are designed strategically.

Public speaking is a way of life for the C-suite, and that is the emphasis of Chapter Four. Some executives are proficient presenters, others not so much. That's why this chapter digs into strategies to help them improve. A word of disclosure: It is not the full treatment given in my first book, *The Truth About Public Speaking: The Three Keys to Great Presentations*, which covered this topic exclusively and comprehensively. Still, given its importance to your communications strategy, a discussion here is warranted.

Some communications shops ignore their government relations cousins. Bad move, for the two functions are intertwined. In an attempt to break down those barriers, Chapter Five examines your advocacy efforts. Whether your C-suite leaders testify on Capitol Hill, before the state legislature, or at a meeting of the local planning and zoning board, you cannot afford to omit a strategic approach. As I told CBS News when they interviewed me in advance of Facebook CEO Mark Zuckerberg's debut Congressional testimony, testifying before Congress is the most important business meeting you will ever have (and yes, I discuss his performance as a case study for how – and how not – to execute strategy when confronting policymakers).

In Chapter Six, we get to the heart of the matter: Sustained professional development leads to life as an influencer. Lifelong learning is a must for any executive seeking to influence their public. This chapter points out that it does not always need to mean large chunks of time. It unveils why sustained programs are necessary and outlines strategies that won't suck all the time from your schedule.

Chapter Seven delves into the importance of training as a vital part of your communications strategy. This applies whether your C-suite is facing the press, stakeholder audiences, or public officials. Finding ways of encouraging sustained professional development is what smart companies do, both for the success of the business and its executives.

Messaging matters, so that's why Chapter Eight is devoted to that vital topic. Among the strategic advice here: What elements many messages lack, and how you can structure your message to capture them, giving you an edge over your rivals. Plus, we offer a case study of what to do when an unexpected event tosses a grenade into your well-planned communications strategy.

Risk is the bane of many C-suite executives. Chapter Nine lifts the lid on the importance of evaluating reputational risk as part of your strategic communications efforts. Some businesses have blinders on, considering only financial risk. Yet it is even more difficult in some circumstances to recover from a hit to your reputation.

Crisis communications forms the basis of Chapter Ten. Every business has its crises, and your communications strategy must take them into account. Note that the emphasis here is on how to communicate in the midst of a disaster, a factor sometimes minimized in the hubbub of an overall crisis plan.

No single work – this volume included – can cover every facet of every topic. That's why you'll find a list of recommended reading. There is some good work out there (and some that is questionable; always vet your sources). I've curated the list so you don't have to. Of course, if you have any suggested additions, I urge you to let me know.

Think of *A+ Strategies for C-Suite Communications: Turning Today's Leaders into Tomorrow's Influencers* as the starting point for your discussions with your C-suite leadership. To spur ongoing dialogue, the conclusion of each chapter contains questions designed to get everyone on your team thinking about your communications strategy and how you can improve your execution of it over the long run. Ignore those questions at your peril. Indeed, they represent one of the greatest values of this book.

This volume intends to encourage improvement. Throughout the pages, C-suite leaders and those who advise them will benefit from insights, techniques, and knowledge I've been fortunate enough to accumulate over many years (with thanks to those who have guided me to that wisdom). It is intended to be an enjoyable journey. My firm belief is that any type of learning that lacks an element of fun is not worth pursuing.

Let's start transforming your leaders into influencers.

Ed Barks
October 2018

CHAPTER 1

COMMUNICATIONS STRATEGY

Good communication is no luxury in today's competitive global marketplace. A solid strategy using all the tools at your disposal wisely, qualifies as a business survival skill.

The fact is your C-suite influencers are sometimes their own worst enemy. As the classic comic strip character Pogo lamented, "We have met the enemy and he is us." Part of your role as a trusted advisor involves delivering frank advice on communications strategy to company leaders. Someone must muster the courage to lay the cards on the table.

Your issues could range from your CEO's prized garish tie to a bad hairstyle to a penchant to talk about the negative rather than the positive. Someone needs to be open and straightforward if your leaders are to attain communications success. That someone can be you – a senior communications or government relations executive. Yes, you will sometimes incur their wrath. On the flip side, you stand to gain credit for guiding their improvement, increasing your influence as a result.

Speaking Truth to Your C-suite

There is no sugar-coating things. You are going to be delivering some sensitive – and in some cases very personal – critiques, news that many of your fellow staffers dare not raise with the boss (perhaps for fear of losing their jobs).

Granted, not every leader is receptive. Some get defensive. Not all have the capability to become influencers. I have observed too many business executives, scientific thought leaders, celebrities, and others deny the need for sustained professional development in the areas of public speaking, media relations, and advocacy. It is a fact of life that some CEOs refuse to acknowledge that their communications skills could use a tune-up.

With some, it is a matter of vanity. They fear they will be viewed as weak if they reach out for assistance. I do not understand this thought process, but it is very real in some businesses. If you encounter this roadblock, turn things around by appealing to that vanity. Let's face it, your C-suite denizens did not achieve their current lofty posts without healthy egos. Use it to your advantage.

Some just want to hog the limelight. It's frustrating when you lay the groundwork and others get the accolades. When it comes to your C-suite, you often have to subsume your ego. "There are two kinds of people," said former Indian Prime Minister Indira Gandhi, "those who do the work and those who take the credit. Try to be in the first group; there is less competition there."

Position the need for ongoing professional development by telling your leaders that they are nurturing an increasingly high public profile. What was good enough for them as managers is no longer good enough for their new, more visible roles. Their prestige merits some individual attention.

Communications pros often find they break down barriers when they talk about the personal benefits executives stand to gain when they become better communicators. What specific personal benefits might they earn by honing those abilities?

- Boost their leadership profiles within your industry and beyond.
- Inspire employees, customers, members, and investors.
- Leapfrog others on the career ladder.
- Enhance opportunities for professional advancement.
- Dodge the embarrassment of poor performance during a high-stakes speech.
- Demonstrate confidence when speaking in public.
- Get rid of trembling voice and knocking knees.
- Keep from wandering aimlessly when delivering presentations.
- Take charge when dealing with any audience.
- Control the flow of media interviews.
- Refuse to fall into reporters' tricks and traps.
- Gain a reputation as a public policy expert.

- Sharpen nonverbal tools for maximum advantage.
- Steer clear of being misunderstood or "misquoted."
- Assume control when question and answer time arrives.
- Conquer distracting nonverbal tendencies.

Responsibility for improvement rests not only with you as a communications professional. In the words of management guru W. Edwards Deming, "Quality is everyone's responsibility." Executives are also personally accountable to their firms. When they signed on to the job, they took a vow to make it a better place. The focus may be on improving things financially, cleaning up from a previous leadership that left a horrible workplace environment, integrating recent acquisitions, increasing community involvement, or any number of other objectives.

Your arguments prove more persuasive in the corner offices when you show that your company also reaps rewards from a more polished leadership. Sell that improvement by emphasizing examples, like these organizational advantages:

- Block rivals from stealing your customers.
- Position your business front and center in the minds of your public.
- Develop and reinforce magnetic organizational messages.
- Prepare for a crisis.
- Save time by hammering out messages and preparing in advance.
- Gain an edge on the competition.
- Decrease the odds that your next product launch will be a dud.
- Instill organizational discipline among those charged with delivering your messages.
- Offer ongoing professional development opportunities to C-suite members for their dealings with the public or press.
- Inspire greater confidence in the public and in your markets during media interviews.

When I speak on the subject of motivating the boss to groups of communications and public affairs experts, I emphasize a leader's obligation to their organization to become a better communicator. Highlighting the above benefits drives that point home. You can do it, too.

It's Not Who You Know, It's Who Knows You

Your company's reputation, its messaging, and its ability to influence your target audiences all depend upon how they perceive you. It's not enough for you to identify with them. They must be able to identify with you.

To raise your profile, you must be able to communicate at peak efficiency. Consider your answers to the following questions to gauge your performance:

- Are you seeking to further leverage your public profile to gain a competitive advantage?

- Is your communications staff overwhelmed and overworked?

- Are you confused about how you can integrate your media relations, public speaking, and public policy efforts?

- Are your government relations and communications teams constantly squabbling?

- Do your executives intimidate your communications staff, preventing the flow of candid advice?

- Are you looking to gain more of a bump from your leaders' speeches and presentations?

- Do your spokespeople even know that written messages exist?

- Do you have multiple locations that need to integrate their public outreach efforts?

Some businesses lack the resources to deal with these strategic and tactical communications issues on their own. They need a sound strategy and powerful tactics, but, for whatever reasons, struggle to get there. Sometimes it takes an external push to help formulate organizational outreach strategies and lifelong learning plans for key individuals. That's okay. Smart businesses realize that you need to get it done, no matter how.

To Define, Not Divide

Communications strategy can be a squishy term. What does it mean? How do you get it? What do you do with it once it's in hand?

Let us follow a modified version of a pattern set forth by Otto Lerbinger in *Corporate Public Affairs: Interacting with Interest Groups, Media, and Government*:

- **Goals** are aspirational and directional; they show where your company wants to go. Consider them as your specific destination on a roadmap.
- **Objectives** put some specifics on those goals. They are both precise and measurable.

- **Tactic**s are what you use to get you to your goals. Think of tactics as the vehicle that will take you on your journey.
- **Strategy** defines how you will attain your goals. This is the map itself that displays main roads, side streets, and points of interest along your route.

Your communications strategy should set forth the general direction your company plans to take. It needs to support your communications outreach to your public and integrate with your overall corporate goals. A properly crafted communications strategy keeps you out of the ruts. It's easy to fall victim to the old saw, "We've always done it that way." That's fine if you're content to manufacture buggy whips or 8-track tape players, losing your shirt in the process. The rest of us are well advised to take a cold, hard look at the current realities, make the tough decisions, and execute them decisively.

Communications and government affairs executives realize all too well that their domains are viewed as tactical or functional – disseminate the message and gain favorable publicity. This means that some organizations neglect these two areas of expertise when making strategic decisions. An effective communications staff should serve as an early warning system, identifying issues just over the horizon that stand to significantly impact their company. The C-suite needs to view this as enormously beneficial in analyzing which direction they need to take.

Always set your strategy before you even begin to consider tactics. Strategy dictates tactics, not the other way around. Sadly, many companies make a beeline for tactics first. If I had the proverbial nickel for every time I've heard something like, "Let's put out a news release" or "How come we're not on Instagram?" I could buy that Mediterranean villa.

Beware phrases like these. They are not your friends. This is purely a tactical approach. Maybe they make sense, maybe not. You cannot know until you see how and if they fit into your communications strategy.

In this case, it's the destination, not the journey, that matters. The outcome of this mistake is normally a fragmented, diffuse approach that provides poor results.

The Long and Winding Road

The journey to a solid communications strategy is long and often complex. You're not going to get it done in a single session or by sitting alone in a room waiting for divine inspiration. It starts with a single step – your analysis. Then you move on to establishing your goals, mapping your strategy, and so forth. Sadly, with many companies even that first step is long overdue.

Strategy represents the big picture. That's why in client work I try to tie your strategy to your business and public policy goals. Some companies get it; some don't. Indeed, some don't even have a well-thought-out communications strategy; this group definitely doesn't get it.

Understandably, many businesses are reluctant to share their strategies in public. Foremost, they fear that rivals will gain an advantage. In addition, unrealistic expectations may arise if they fail to meet their targets. They may also be working on the assumption that their target audience has a good grasp on the issue. This is rarely the case. In fact, your messaging should include a dose of context to ensure everyone understands the issue.

The question becomes, how do you assemble a communications strategy? Here's a quick-start approach. Analysis comes first. Examine the environment in which you operate. Gauge your market, competitors, and other stakeholders such as your clients or customers, local community, labor force, and vendors. If you operate in a regulated industry, be sure to include your oversight bodies, too.

Next, blue sky your strategic options. Everything is on the table at this stage. Even the silliest sounding idea may contain a kernel of wisdom. Once you've exhausted the idea factory, evaluate the ideas and choose which opportunities are likely to serve you best.

With those decisions made, it is vital that you spell out the role communications and government relations will play. This is where it is vital to do your spade work ahead of time. You must ensure that your C-suite understands the importance of having your skill set involved from the start. Spell out what role communications staff is to play, the tactics to be deployed, and the steps the company as a whole will take to implement the strategy. Bear in mind that the C-suite's interests rest with the larger picture. They are responsible for the entire company. To take your seat at the decision-making table, you need to work from that same perspective.

Outline in clear and concise terms what is expected of your C-suite, too. Here, you need to determine how best to couch this message. Some executives will be receptive; others may balk. "Many receive advice, only the wise profit from it," noted author Harper Lee.

For this to succeed, you need to employ experienced communications pros capable of thinking – and acting – strategically. Your C-suite will shut you out of executing your strategy if your staff proves ignorant, inexperienced, or indifferent. And they will be justified in doing so.

Of course, evaluation also needs to be considered. Don't wait until after your campaign is over to assess your performance. Check your progress along the way. Make sure that your strategic document explicitly states how and when you plan to analyze. Here's an important point: Refuse to get hung up on numbers. While some things can be measured and quantified, not everything can be put into neat little boxes. Indeed, you might overlook some basic factors if all you see are numbers. Go beyond where many organizations go by examining such difficult things to measure as reputational aspects and the effect on your public policy goals. More on this in a few moments.

Fighting the Good Fight

For now, let's take the example of a public affairs campaign in which your firm is aiming to enact legislation. Your battle plan might look something like this, as suggested by Lerbinger:

- **Analysis of the state of affairs.** This can cover such issues as which organizations oppose your stance, those lawmakers who support or oppose you, and any previous legislative efforts.

- **Your company's goals for the campaign.** Is enacting a new law realistic? Or might you be better off trying to block bad legislation? Can you assemble a coalition to strengthen your voice and political reach?

- **Strategy.** As noted above, this is the section that outlines how you plan to achieve your goals.

- **Target markets.** Certainly, legislators are part of the picture. You also need to consider what segments of the public need to hear your message and perhaps act on it.

- **Messaging.** Any communications or public policy campaign without a message is destined to lose. Your messages must be elegant and magnetic (see Chapter Seven for more on messaging).

- **Communication vehicles.** Perhaps you'll reach out to key policymakers one-on-one. You might use digital media ads to reach a certain slice of your target audience. A traditional media campaign might work, or you might send your C-suite on a speaking tour.

- **Timing.** Spell out a timeline, right down to the specific steps you need to take to gain success. For instance, have legislative hearings been scheduled on your issue? If so, back track from that date to determine what you need to do when.

- **Budget**. Marshal your resources, both in terms of finances and personnel. Note that, while this is one of the later strategic considerations, many a client's first question concerns budget. While somewhat understandable (you don't want to waste your time looking at Jaguars if you can only afford a Ford), starting your decision-making process here is very much a cart before the horse method.

- **Assessment**: To succeed in the future, you need to judge how you've performed in the past, so make it a point to do so every step of the way. Bear in mind that assessment involves more than numeric measurements. You've got to examine aspects like reputational and public policy success, too.

Be sure never to over-promise when devising your communications strategy. You look like a winner when you outperform your objectives. If you fall short by even a small margin, you'll be labeled as big a loser as the 1962 New York Mets.

The All-powerful, All-knowing C-suite Executive

The perception exists that by the time executives ascend to the C-suite they are omniscient and all powerful.

- Financial expertise? You bet.
- Savvy at dealing with people? Check.
- Working knowledge of legal clashes facing the business? Right.
- Insightful when it comes to the inevitable cyberattack? Yup.
- Herding a board of directors? Sure.
- Expert at communicating with their publics? Got it.
- Public policy professionals? Yes, indeed.

Hold on a second. The most respected CEOs recognize their strengths and challenges. Those with legal backgrounds shine when the law is considered. The financial whiz fully understands that piece of the puzzle. There is often a disconnect, however, when it comes to communications and public policy. Why? The answer is simple. Relatively few CEOs come up through those ranks.

This is not the place to launch into a diatribe on the merits of that tradition. Suffice to say, the fact that they lack grounding in these critical disciplines affects the company in tangible ways. This reality creates problems for the communications or government relations executive who counsels the C-suite:

- You must find a way to gently and diplomatically explain the rules of the road with regard to communicating with external audiences, be they elected officials, reporters, or various stakeholders.
- Viewed as a prophet in your own land, your advice is sometimes tuned out.
- You are responsible for developing and sustaining a professional development program the boss will adhere to.
- Your professional reputation takes a hit whenever your leadership goes rogue.
- As the individual charged with shaping the company's reputation in the marketplace, your standing in the eyes of peers is in play.
- Your continued employment is threatened.
- You suffer sideways glances from co-workers who wonder why you don't seem that good at your job.

C-suite influencers also face risks when they fail to execute – or even to comprehend – the company's communications and public policy objectives. They risk:

- Losing face in the marketplace over a sloppy quote in the press.
- Eroding the board's confidence and trust in them and, in the process, their own job security.
- Failure to gain recognition as an industry thought leader,
- Becoming a well-known laughing stock if they are not prepared for the heat of Q&A during a Congressional hearing. *murder boards*
- Lowering the company's stock price.
- Gaining the perception as a lightweight in the marketplace.

You Think You Have a Problem?

Your C-suite influencers hold in their hands the responsibility for communicating your business' messages. How can you raise your odds for success? First, of course, comes your strategy. A major part of this strategy means ensuring your messages are airtight. Work with your managers and frontline personnel to fine-tune your messaging. A note of caution: Don't let them drag you into the weeds. They lack the bigger picture view that you've attained. It's up to you to test the overarching effectiveness of your message.

Next, get C-suite buy-in for your strategy. Granted, this can be easier said than done. If you are a respected veteran of your firm's communications battles – playing General Grant to your CEO's Abraham Lincoln – you have likely banked plenty of reputational capital (a term introduced, as best I can determine, by Charles J. Fombrun in *Reputation: Realizing Value from the Corporate Image*). If, however, you are newer or find yourself teetering on the brink of mistrust, you have some work to do.

Find some victories. Start small and build your credibility over time. For example, maybe your first step is to secure an interview for your CEO with a relatively friendly trade publication. Make sure they see the article with their quotes highlighted. Use that to segue into a seemingly informal discussion of your messaging. Eventually, you'll work your way up to counseling them for that make or break Congressional testimony appearance.

External consultants can be helpful in this regard. The good ones want you to shine. As a consultant, sure, I'm pleased to bask in reflected glory. Yet I always maintain the full understanding that I am there to make your business – and you – look good.

Consultants can also serve as a bridge to your C-suite. They should be experienced at massaging sometimes massive egos and, when necessary, laying down the law. In plain terms, if it comes down to it, isn't it better that the CEO gives them the boot rather than you?

Tactically, a media training workshop may be a good idea. Or, if you are facing a public policy issue, Congressional testimony preparation is likely in order. Whatever the proper direction, make sure you turn to an experienced pro with sufficient gravitas in the eyes of your C-suite.

Here's one great idea I got from a colleague. One of the symptoms of his problem: A C-suite executive in his company asked to review before publication an article in which he was to be quoted. Anyone with a modicum of background in American media relations knows that is taboo (though in many international markets it is permitted). My colleague's idea? Offer a workshop for the entire C-suite that gives them the rules of the road. This allows for an open dialogue on the subject. Plus, inviting the entire C-suite avoids obvious targeting of one individual, which can lead to an uncomfortable situation for all involved.

The Reluctant Communicator: A Strategy for Improvement

Let us now turn to two questions that prove perplexing for many organizations. First, why do C-suite influencers, board members, and issue experts need to master communications skills? Second, how can you encourage the reluctant executives among you to improve?

An answer to the first question seems patently obvious. Superior communications skills are essential if you want to avoid public embarrassment and achieve success, both on an individual and an organizational level.

There are countless examples of forums that can make or break you: A speech to an audience that includes key customers, an interview on CNN, a presentation to the board of directors, unveiling research to a professional society, a new product launch, and addressing a press gaggle during a crisis, just to name a few.

Moving on to question number two, determining how to motivate them to take that voyage can be akin to navigating whitewater rapids. Some executives are supremely confident in their ability to deliver a magnetic message. But that confidence is sometimes misplaced. You may have encountered this type of "know-it-all" boss. When the idea of training to sharpen their skills comes up, they squash the discussion with a clever phrase like, "I already know how to talk."

This reluctance is often nothing more than a mask for fear. Then again, as Supreme Court Justice Sonia Sotomayor says, "A surplus of effort could overcome a deficit of confidence." I want to share with you other methods by which I motivate my clients who may enter into a public situation with some trepidation. You can use the same techniques with your C-suite.

First, it is important to forge respect right from the start. We've all heard how crucial the first 30 seconds of any interaction are. "(W)ith live entertainment, people let you know right then and there. That relationship is established in 30 seconds. The first 30 seconds, they'll let you know whether they like you or not," maintains comedian Tracy Morgan. During that phase, the reluctant participant sizes up her opposite. If you approach the conversation with a take charge attitude, you are more likely to earn respect.

Second, maintaining an assertive yet diplomatic demeanor is a key to success. When I work with hard-chargers, I realize they are used to getting their own way. Leaders smell any hint of fear right away. The result? They quickly lose interest, patience, and respect. Their reluctance quotient shoots sky high. You need to be viewed as a trusted advisor, not a mere hired hand.

Third, expertise is crucial. You must realistically assess whether you and your team are up to the job. If you lack communications strategy or training experience, it is well worth budgeting for a veteran consultant familiar with strategies capable of overcoming reluctance.

Fourth, I use the principle of ju jitsu, the martial art in which you use your opponent's strength to your own advantage. Let me tell you the story of the time I worked with a celebrity who made it clear that he knew all there was to know about talking with reporters; he was a most reluctant participant. I let him become the star of the show (a role to which he was accustomed), letting him guide his less experienced workshop partner. My role became one of maintaining the flow, tightening up loose ends, and gently correcting any misinformation that arose. Did it work? You bet. I had the opportunity to work with that same celebrity a few months later. This time, there was a level of trust. He was much more relaxed and much more willing to let me do my job. The three of us in the room worked in perfect harmony preparing for their upcoming media campaign.

The issue of why leaders need to develop strong communications skills is easy to tackle. It's that next step – advising the reluctant on how they can improve – that separates the pro from the amateur.

Not Everything Can Be Measured

Time and again, I have found it difficult to get companies to understand the benefits attached to strengthening their communications capabilities. They want results driven to the financial bottom line. Not everything works like that.

There is more at stake than dollars and cents. Reputation matters. Factors like the public's perception of your company's management and its performance, the credibility of your C-suite, and the trustworthiness and competence of your CEO come into play.

It's easier to define quantity than quality. Measuring quality is akin to then-Supreme Court Justice Potter Stewart commenting on pornography: "I know it when I see it." So why would C-suite decision-makers go through the hassle of even trying to calculate reputation? Reason one: Their jobs in years to come will depend on it. Who needs them if we can simply plug in a few numbers and arrive at a result?

The financial and sales people have it easy. The financial bottom line is a straightforward number. Sales also shows a specific, inviolable number. Proving how much communications or government relations contributes to the bottom line is a much trickier proposition.

But those numbers cannot measure reputation. Some public affairs and public relations agencies have magic black box formulas that claim to divine accurate measurements for the work they do. If this is the case, I've often wondered why everyone's formula is different and proprietary.

In *The Tyranny of Metrics*, author Jerry Z. Muller clarifies the picture. He serves up an excellent argument about the unwise approach to measuring everything:

- " ... what can be measured is not always what is worth measuring; what gets measured may have no relationship to what we really want to know. The costs of measuring may be greater than the benefits ... And measurement may provide us with distorted knowledge – knowledge that seems solid but is actually deceptive."

- " ... accountability has come to mean demonstrating success through standardized measurement, as if only that which can be counted really counts."
- "Above all, measurement may become counterproductive when it tries to measure the unmeasurable and quantify the unquantifiable."

Gaming the System

He also notes that metrics are easy to finagle. This may explain the variance in the black box formulas discussed above. "Whenever reward is tied to measured performance," the author writes, "metric fixation invites gaming."

Unfortunately, this metric fixation has become standard operating procedure in the corporate C-suite (and in the non-profit world, too, for that matter). Executives who refuse to bow down to the god of numbers are frozen out by peers. Even some communications executives have been steamrolled into abiding by this wrong-headed scheme.

Expertise used to mean amassing knowledge in a specific field. Now, however, the accountants and "measurers" have taken over (and don't get me started on how my favorite sport – baseball – has been taken over by the statheads).

How have we allowed this to happen? My speculation is that we now have so much artificial capacity to crunch numbers that we feel compelled to use it (if you doubt how reliant our brains have become, ask a colleague or your kids to add up or multiply some simple numbers in their heads; good luck getting correct answers).

As Muller writes, "(N)umbers are valued precisely because they replace reliance on the subjective, experienced-based judgments of those in power." Does this mean today's corporate decision-makers are dumber than ever? Not likely. But it does mean that much of their license to think – to arrive at strategic, analytical judgments – has been stripped.

Some corporate CEOs agree. "I don't like making decisions with analytics," says Nvidia CEO Jensen Huang, as quoted in Adam Bryant's *The Corner Office* "I actually like making decisions with intuition. I like to validate the decision with analytics. I don't believe you can analyze your way into success. I think it's too complicated."

Admittedly, larger businesses have a harder time shunning the fixation with numbers. It is challenging for the C-suite to gain a clear ground-level view. This makes decisions based purely on numbers attractive.

Follow the Money

There is one business segment that understandably fans the flames of this obsession with metrics – those who make their living from collecting and evaluating data. While one colleague of mine who runs an analytics consultancy concedes that there is more to it than just numbers, he does get a bit touchy when the discussion digs too deep.

Our metric-centric business climate means that non-financial and intrinsic factors are ignored. Did your chief communications officer just place your CEO on the network evening news? Sorry, there's no number attached to that, so we can't factor that in. Has your chief technology officer just made an important connection with a high-profile customer after speaking on a panel, a situation that could result in an enhanced reputation for your company? Tough, there's no numerical value there.

The point is metrics are a poor and unreliable substitute for C-suite judgment. Moreover, they divert resources from long-term goals, which explains our tragic fixation with quarterly results as opposed to more meaningful long-range performance (to say nothing of other goals in the realms of reputation, social responsibility, and public policy).

Yes, profits matter. But other important factors like reputation, market share, customer satisfaction, and worker morale underlie those profits and can serve as springboards to ongoing innovation, something mere numbers cannot do.

Weighing the Wrong Stuff

One financial expert with whom I discussed this topic told me in no uncertain terms that he can compute reputational damage by noting the market valuation lost after a crisis. While I can by no means claim fiscal expertise, I believe that market valuation – and the stock markets' capricious mood swings – are poor yardsticks of the economy and of individual companies, to say nothing of its failure to serve as a valid reputation barometer.

Do you remember the phrase "voodoo economics" from a long-ago presidential campaign? That's my view of such measurement attempts. Futility reigns. The solution? Trust the executives who have demonstrated wisdom and experience in making decisions on such matters.

This is not to say we are left to toss darts at a dartboard, to merely guess at the effect of reputational risk. Fortunately, there are other means of assessment.

Consider this recommendation from Robert G. Eccles, Scott C. Newquist, and Roland Schatz from their article "Reputation and Its Risks" in the *Harvard Business Review*.

"Various techniques exist for evaluating a company's reputation. They include media analysis, surveys of stakeholders (customers, employees, investors, NGOs) and industry executives, focus groups, and public opinion polls. Although all are useful, a detailed and structured analysis of what the media are saying is especially important because the media shape the perceptions and expectations of all stakeholders."

Another alternative method of measurement comes our way courtesy of the U.S. military's "after action review." Such reviews generally concentrate on these questions:

- What was expected to take place?
- What really happened?
- Why was a difference observed (or not)?
- What can we do to achieve a better outcome in the future?

The paper "Organizational Dynamics: A Focus for Effective Risk Management" chimes in with such best practices as making simulation drills a part of the planning process. It also preaches the wisdom of activating your company's risk committee, or forming one if none currently exists (author's note: You would be wise to give your chief communications officer a seat at that table). Your communicators should also create discussions surrounding reputational risks that may appear on the horizon (as I've said many a time – to many a sideways glance – if your current communications staff is incapable of this, get rid of them and bring on board more capable minds).

Getting Paid to Make Hard Choices

What other steps can you take to manage reputational risk effectively? The Federal Reserve Bank of Philadelphia offers some key elements for banks to consider:

"Reinforcing a risk management culture by creating awareness at all staff levels

Instilling ethics throughout the organization by enforcing a code of conduct for the board, management, and staff ...

Establishing a crisis management team in the event there is a significant action that may trigger a negative impact on the organization"

If it's good enough for bankers, it ought to be good enough for the rest of the economy, too. You would be wise to weave the Philadelphia Fed's recommendations into your company's reputational risk planning.

The point is not to cave in to an obsession with measuring everything solely in dollar terms. As the above methods point out, reputational risk is a very real phenomenon, one that shrewd organizations and communications executives recognize and respect.

Measurement is not an alternative to judgment. It demands the ability to make qualitative decisions about whether to measure, what to measure, how to evaluate significance, whether there will be rewards and penalties, and who sees the results.

Fold the data into your brain (meaning your literal, human brain, not a spreadsheet of some sort). The C-suite gets paid to make the tough calls. So help them use the wisdom they have carefully cultivated over time.

Muller argues that not all problems can be solved, and even fewer can be solved by metrics. Bravo.

There is no substitute for knowing your subject, which boils down to experience and skill. Never let your C-suite take its eye off that ball. Once that is lost, why would we need a C-suite? We'll just let the numbers do the talking.

Five for the Future

Now that you've read Chapter One, begin to implement the strategic ideas that matter to you. Use these "Five for the Future" discussion questions to help you sustain your C-suite's professional development over the long run. Discuss these issues with co-workers, professional colleagues, mentors, and in your own mind:

1. What steps can you take – or have you already taken – to engender trust with your C-suite?
2. How often do you revisit your strategic communications plan?
3. What about your messages for key issues – when is the last time you reassessed them?
4. How can you start a dialogue about measuring your firm's reputation that goes beyond just the numbers?
5. Evaluate your communications resources. Where do you stand with regard to your staff's capabilities? Where do you need to bolster your assets?

Bonus content

Whether your communications strategy calls for you to raise your C-suite's influence through the media, a public speaking tour, or by dealing with policymakers, I have some extra pointers for you. Log on to www.barkscomm.com/APlusBonus for your free copy of "A Dozen Designs to Raise Your CEO's Profile."

CHAPTER 2

SHAPING A STRATEGIC APPROACH

As Sandra M. Oliver points out in *Handbook of Corporate Communication and Public Relations,* many businesses are moving toward a more decentralized management style. While that is fine under some conditions, consider carefully whether it makes sense for your communications endeavors. A central management approach for communications is advised, especially for those corporations with far-flung global operations.

Every business communicates in some fashion. Some do it consciously, others by the seat of the pants. Some do it well, some are challenged. The key to it all? A solid communications strategy.

A well-thought-out, written communications policy can help turn your business goals into reality. You need to let key audiences know that you exist, what you do, and what you want them to do.

Why take a strategic approach to your communications situation? The benefits are many. Here is but a handful:

- Shinier reputation.
- Increased revenues.
- Influencing opportunities for your C-suite officers.
- Expanded service offerings.
- Better environment for your industry.
- Improved relationships with clients, customers, members, and vendors.

- New client referrals that flow from the alliance you forge with your communications strategy consultant.
- Higher worker morale.
- Boosted stock price for public companies.
- Friendlier government regulation.

Developing and implementing a professional development program that can truly foster communications skills matters. Yours might look something like this, a format based on Oliver's work:

Phase one: Assess your existing communications capabilities. This where you gauge your true capabilities. Consider a series of questions. Be tough and realistic. Is your current staff up to the task? To what extent do you need to work on obtaining C-suite buy in? What about your messaging; is it first-rate or are you starting from ground zero? How does that messaging align with your company's overall business and public policy goals?

Phase two: Test your messaging to see if it stands up to the heat in the hottest kitchen (see Chapter Eight for details). Schedule a series of workshops designed to help your spokespeople internalize and verbalize your messages, and to ramp up their communications skills. These workshops should cover all of the critical areas: Dealing with the media; delivering presentations to a variety of audiences; and dealing with federal, state, and local policymakers. Granted, this is a broad waterfront – another argument as to why you need that overarching strategy. Also during this phase, develop your communications plan. Be sure to include a section of ethics in your plan. Your C-suite must understand (and, it is hoped, strongly support) an ethical approach to your dealings with the outside world.

Phase three: Assess how your communications efforts connect to your business plan. Establish ongoing feedback processes. Without mechanisms that tell you how you're performing, you'll be flying blind. Be sure your processes are written. Distribute them among all of your spokespeople and gain their explicit assent. Anyone who declines to abide by them should be dropped as a spokesperson. They will poison your efforts. In month three, you will also continue the workshops you initiated last month, starting more colleagues on the program and moving those who've already begun into more advanced learning. Finally, measure your results with an emphasis on how your program is impacting your bottom line, both financially and reputationally, and to what degree it is helping you achieve your business and public policy goals. It's important to build your strategy around those goals. Otherwise, it's meaningless.

Brief Is Better

What about the document outlining your strategy? Keep it short (do you really think your CEO has time to ingest a *War and Peace*-like tome?). Moreover, there is no way to anticipate every possible scenario, so think of it as more a set of guidelines than an encyclopedia of hard and fast rules.

Write it as if you were in the real world (you are, you know). Your strategy guidelines are not the place for lofty language often found in fanciful mission statements. It's not pie-in-the-sky theory. Fancy charts are not necessary (unless you need to keep the guy who loves creating fancy charts and graphics busy). Your aim is to create a working guide for your communications endeavors.

And be sure to keep it to communications, not marketing. How communications and marketing ever got lumped together mystifies me. They are two distinct disciplines.

Who should be involved? Interview your CEO and your entire communications staff, including administrative personnel. While the top dog may have the big picture view when it comes to the communications function (though that's not always the case), it is vital to gain intelligence from the individuals responsible for implementing your plans. Ask them about the problems and risks they see, and about the successes and opportunities. A junior staffer may well have a brilliant idea that has failed to gain traction. Considering it during your strategy sessions can help raise its profile, perhaps benefiting your company.

It's often wise to bring in a consultant for a couple of reasons. First, it gives you an outside perspective you may otherwise miss. Second, it can be difficult for internal staff to raise certain issues. An experienced consultant is not afraid of initiating such challenging conversations.

Some companies try to get by with the argument, "But our VP of communications knows all this stuff cold." Fine. If she is hit by the proverbial bus tomorrow, where does that leave your communications efforts? A written document helps keep everyone on the same wavelength. Will there be some who don't understand or drag their feet? Probably. When you call them on the carpet for neglecting the plan, you'll have something in writing to back you up.

It also serves to keep your external communications clear and consistent. Think of your strategy as your North Star. If you start to drift off course, it can painlessly help you make any obligatory mid-course corrections.

One of the first and most important steps is figuring out your target audiences. Consider such factors as level of seniority, geography, gender, age, occupation, and education when targeting those you want to reach.

Many other dynamics can also come into play. The point is you need to ascertain which aspects are most relevant to your efforts.

Assess the 1s and 5s

Using the 1 through 5 categorizations above, map out where your targets – customers, community leaders, service providers, stockholders, rivals, and more – fall. Then approach them accordingly.

List your competitors and offer a quick look at their communications capabilities. You may find weak areas of theirs that you can exploit, or determine strengths of theirs that you should tiptoe around.

Messaging is a critical part of your communications strategy (much more on this in Chapter Eight). If you lack written messages, integrate their formation into your strategic process. If you have them in hand already, congratulations. Just be sure to review them regularly to ensure they remain up to date.

A sustained communications training program may also be in order – for example:

- A media training schedule for executives who face the press.
- A series on effective public speaking for those who deliver presentations, both external and internal.
- A public policy component that demonstrates how to deal with Congressional testimony and grassroots advocacy efforts.

You should also spell out the tools and tactics deemed most appropriate for various situations (A note of caution: Never try to short circuit the process by deciding on tactics first). Maybe a series of Facebook posts makes sense, maybe not. Maybe a news conference is the way to go, maybe not. Maybe you want to send your CEO to visit far-flung operations, maybe not. You can't know until you devise your strategy, messaging, and target markets.

All of which brings us to your communications budget. Only you can know what level of spending best suits your business. My advice here is to make this a conscious decision. With your business objectives in mind, prioritize, then decide what makes sense for you from a budgetary point of view.

Assess your strategy's performance often, especially after big events. These might include interviews with key reporters, your CEO's upcoming speaking tour, or a round of Congressional testimony.

Schedule regular reviews of your strategy, too. The interval depends on your level of activity. If you focus on only one or two relatively static issues, semi-annually may be fine. If you keep a lot of irons in the fire or are confronting a crisis, reassessment on a daily or even an hourly basis may be necessary.

One final point that drives my data-oriented colleagues nuts: Communications strategy is far more an art than a science. If you go in search of tools that claim to quantify your progress, expect frustration. It takes diligent work and brainpower, not some random system that spits out a score of 4.33 on a scale of 5.

Never forget: Your communications strategy must be a pillar of your long-term business goals. Build it, nurture it, and implement it.

A Strategy Before Tactics Case Study

I once had the pleasure of participating in an organizational planning session. A few dozen of the company's best and brightest packed into a room to contemplate the coming year and how to best advance the firm's goals.

Participants put forth lots of valuable ideas, tossing out thoughts so fast and furious the scribe could barely keep pace. It all boiled down to how to communicate the organization's value more broadly and forcefully. Among the notions: Let's reach out more through digital media channels. Let's retweet each other to expand the organization's reach. Let's work to establish more collaborations across sometimes disparate parts of the organization. These ideas were all well and good.

Do you notice a vital missing component? Right, there was no hat tip toward a robust communications strategy. It was akin to sitting in the White House situation room and charging into war before considering less drastic options. It sounds great at first blush to throw some tactics and techniques against a wall to see what sticks. The fact remains if you lack strategy you will lack success.

My fear is that all these bright, dedicated folks will now go about their merry way doing their own thing. The result will be lots of movement with little cohesive forward motion.

The lesson: Whenever you decide to strengthen your communications capabilities, start with the strategy. The tools will make themselves evident once you've set your compass in the right direction. What are some of those tools? Let's take a look.

Look at Me, I'm a Piñata!

As chief communicator for your company, you sometimes need to fall on your sword for the good of the order. Yes, that's true even when you adhere to a sound strategy.

Perhaps the most vivid example of this takes place routinely in the White House briefing room. No matter your political inclinations or your level of respect for the press secretary du jour, it can be instructive to witness how skilled (or in some cases, ham-handed) these high-profile spokespeople are at shielding the boss by keeping reporters largely at bay. I strongly advise that you watch at least a handful of briefings on C-SPAN. They can be highly instructive.

Press secretaries in the administration and on Capitol Hill are accustomed to getting slapped around by the press corps. This serves as a reminder to all communications and government relations executives. There are times when someone in your organization has to play the bull's eye to the media's Robin Hood.

You don't want your CEO taking incoming arrows. They could end up looking bad by refusing to answer questions from the press or by shooting from the lip. Professional communicators realize that this protective detail is all in the line of duty. Furthermore, they know not to take it personally. Reporters don't hate them (well, at least not necessarily). It's part of the business deal between the press and those they cover.

You could make it easier on yourself by throwing open the floodgates to your C-suite or by spinning. Good luck with that.

Look at the results from an organizational point of view when you take the professional route. Keeping the boss out of the line of fire may well preserve their reputation and ease the pressure on your business. True, it might create a slight dent in your image. But not with reporters who understand how the game is played. You stand to gain status when you stick to your position and do so respectfully and professionally.

Let me be clear about one important facet here. None of this is to say that you should hide your C-suite as a matter of course. This is not regular order. It needs to be a strategic decision taken on a case-by-case basis, and implemented only during challenging times.

You can often have impact on turning down the heat from your current flap, at least for a day. By then, your kerfuffle may be long forgotten, thanks to today's minute by minute news cycle. Don't you think that earns you some credit and admiration from your C-suite?

More than Talking Pretty

The notion of thinking strategically is one of the hardest things to get across with regard to your C-suite's professional development initiatives. A good program means more than learning how to talk to reporters, deliver presentations, or offer persuasive Congressional testimony.

While all those things are important, every one of those communications efforts feeds into (or at least should feed into) a larger objective. It may be a public policy goal, a desire for more sales, a shinier reputation, or any number of other possibilities. As Ben Franklin said, "Tell me and I forget. Teach me and I remember. Involve me and I learn."

Often, when I get a call about a project, the prospective client says something like, "We have a new product, and our key spokespeople need media training." That's a good start. But it is sometimes difficult to shift the conversation to the larger, more meaningful focus. In this case, that might be something like, "Our company's reputation and its financial well-being demand a successful launch."

Here are some other examples:

- **What I hear**: "Our CEO has never had media training and needs to be better in front of the press."
- **What the conversation is actually about**: The big guy blew a recent interview that took the company's stock price down a peg or two. Our future success depends on his ability to sharpen his communications edge.
- **What I hear**: "Our production team will be delivering a series of presentations to key audiences, and they need to improve their public speaking skills."
- **What the conversation is actually about**: We recently experienced a problem with our manufacturing process that left our customers in the lurch. We have fences to mend in order to continue meeting our revenue projections.
- **What I hear**: "Our messaging needs some work."
- **What the conversation is actually about**: Every time we go up against the competition, we get our brains beat in. Our people don't know what to say or how to say it. As a result, we keep losing accounts and misfiring on our sales targets.
- **What I hear**: "Can you work with our president before she testifies before a Congressional Committee?"
- **What the conversation is actually about**: We've been fighting this public policy battle for years and the key Congressional committee has finally decided to hold hearings on the issue. We'll be set back forever if we miss this opportunity.

Why is this important? I'm going to assume that you are not in the business of churning out flawless communicators. Your business purpose is likely loftier than that, perhaps bringing healthier foods to the masses or even curing cancer. So start with your goals, then decide how and when your professional development activities fit in. The next time you consider professional development surrounding your communications efforts, be clear about why you are doing it. There has to be more than making your executives talk pretty. This crucial communications endeavor must mesh with your overall business goals. In fact, if you cannot tie your communications strategy to such goals, you are wasting precious budget dollars.

How Professional Service Firms Benefit from Communications Strategy

This perspective also applies to professional service firms. Some still undertake business development the same, old way they've always done it. Ask for client referrals, speak before the local Kiwanis Club on the rubber chicken circuit, even (shudder!) make cold calls. All of those approaches are fine and can be part of a viable strategy (well, maybe not cold calling, but that's fodder for another forum).

Competition is fierce in the professional service ranks. These firms pursue new clients with a vengeance and do their best to hold on to current buyers. That's why smart firms poised to zoom ahead in the 21st century use another method: Forging alliances with consultants who work with a similar clientele.

These service firms may concentrate on several areas of the business. Among them:

- Accounting
- Law
- Commercial real estate
- Banking
- Design
- Architecture
- Engineering

Regardless of their area of specialization, there is a common thread each of their clients has when it comes to their bottom line: The need for a convincing, cohesive communications strategy. Why is that the tie that binds? Let's examine:

Accounting: It is vital that a company's executives have the ability to explain in clear language their financial picture to their boards and, as appropriate, to staff and external audiences. This is doubly true for firms that provide audit services. In addition, public companies must know how to deliver the numbers not only with clarity, but also with ethics in mind. The lack of a communications strategy here could be a killer.

Law: Top lawyers realize that much of the legal battle is fought – and won or lost – in the court of public opinion. Relying on a strictly legal argument is not always the winning move. A smart communications strategy bolsters the legal case.

Commercial real estate: These professional service firms have multiple audiences that scream for information, among them investors, planning board members, community activists impacted by a development, builders, architects, and more. In fact, in my 20 years of experience as a consultant, I have found this type of firm to have among the most diverse – and therefore most challenging – scope of target audiences. If they fail to create and adhere to a rigorous communications strategy, their investors may soon wave goodbye and the regulators may stop granting permits.

Banking: Both the mega-banks and smaller community banks exist in a hugely competitive environment. With banks now offering a dizzying array of services, the value of their services and their ability to deliver them must be clear in the minds of potential customers. A coherent communications strategy is the only way to get there.

Design: Strategy and messaging can be challenging for design agencies. The reason? Their leaders are highly visual. Thus, communicating in words may not be a strength. More than some others on this list, design firms would be wise to call in a communications strategy consultant to help ensure their stellar visual messaging matches its verbal counterpart.

Architecture: These experts should have a ready grasp of the need for communications strategy. After all, their livelihood depends on designing structures that are safe and sturdy. Your business' message should be much the same – able to withstand the strongest winds and impervious to the heaviest rains. So find someone who knows how to construct an architecturally elegant message.

Engineering: Math is the prime domain of many an engineer. This means they are often working with the side of the brain opposite of what it takes to communicate. Why bother trying to turn a weakness into a strength? Either hire an experienced communications pro and give him some leeway or, if that's too much of a budget commitment, contract with a consultant who can put together the playbook for you.

Ask Your Accountant to Measure These Assets

The question now becomes, how can you find the right communications strategy consultant? Unlike lawyers, architects, and accountants, you'll not find them in the yellow pages. And an online search primarily dredges up links to one of the Big 5 consulting firms (if you like black box methods and long, incomprehensible tomes written at your expense, be my guest).

My assumption here is that you're looking for a service that is more nimble and focused tightly on your communications needs; one that won't try to upsell and cross sell you to no end. That's where the independent has the advantage. How to find such an authority?

Referrals from trusted colleagues are often the best sources. Ask communications or government relations pros you know who they've worked with in the past to help with their communications strategy. There are not that many legitimate strategists around, so be sure to vet fully those who appear interesting.

Networking among your professional and social circles also comes into play. It could range from a colleague in a related industry to your next door neighbor who serves on the board of a community group. You never know who might be able to recommend the right person.

Digital media may be a good source. Granted, this one can take some digging. Still, invest a little time and keep up with what potential consultants post on their blogs and on LinkedIn. You can also follow them on Twitter if you're not afraid of the drinking from a fire hose effect.

Your involvement in community and volunteer groups can unearth a rich lode of possibilities. Many executives from professional service firms gravitate to such organizations to give back by sharing their expertise. So do communications strategy consultants. That means you can get a firsthand look at their capabilities when working on projects together.

Research to see who has written seriously on communications strategy can also pay off. Those who are serious about their chosen field should be writing and speaking on issues of the day, much as lawyers and architects might. Read and listen to their opinions. As Wernher von Braun said, "Research is what I'm doing when I don't know what I'm doing."

Now comes the hard part for many professional service practitioners: Reach out and begin to establish relationships with a small handful of communications strategists. Gauge your comfort level. Not every strategist is a good fit for every firm. For example, some consultants prefer to deal with Fortune 1000 corporations, others with small non-profits. Some may be a good cultural fit for your firm, others may be too laid back or too "in your face." And sometimes it boils down to the vibe you get.

The point is if you are responsible for growth and client development at a law firm, accounting practice, architects' office, or any number of other professional service firms, it's time to bolster your communications strategy. It's a good deal for you and your clients.

Winning Executive Buy-in: A Case Study

Let us close this chapter with a question I received from an executive with responsibility for her organization's communications endeavors. As the result of longstanding efforts to capture the attention of her C-suite executives, she finally got them to commit to a day-long meeting to hammer out their communications goals.

She was seeking advice on how to structure the day to win buy-in for her plans. Her plan was to begin with a thorough review of the organization's current communications undertakings, its available resources, and what similar organizations were doing on the communications front.

This immediately raised some red flags in my mind. First, the entire focus seemed to be on talking as opposed to listening. Gaining acceptance from any crowd involves a dialogue, yet her plans hinted at a monologue.

Second, senior executives tend to have low tolerance for lectures. A lengthy sermon, complete with slides, may be fine for some audiences (though experience tells me that this type of audience is dwindling given today's era of shortened attention spans). For this C-suite group, it's best to keep an eye on actively involving them in a genuine way right from the start. Beginning with a comprehensive review could well lead them to walk out or, at best, tune out. This interactivity must quickly and meaningfully go to the heart of the communications plan. That is, none of those cutesy and uber-annoying "icebreaking" exercises.

Third, these are pretty smart people or they would not have attained their senior positions. So make use of their expertise and their strong personalities. The more you can make them think your ideas are their ideas, the more support you will win. Our executive's goal should be not to make them suffer through a windy review, but to find ways to transform them into advocates for the desired communications goals and budget.

Fourth, consider the session's facilitator. She (or another internal team member) is not the best candidate. An external consultant is able to guide the conversation with a firmer hand and in her chosen direction.

The crux of the matter: Get C-suite executives involved as active participants in the decision-making process if you hope to increase the odds of gaining their support and turning them into proponents of your communications goals.

Five for the Future

Now that you've read Chapter Two, begin to implement the strategic ideas that matter to you. Use these "Five for the Future" discussion questions to help you sustain your C-suite's professional development over the long run. Discuss these issues with co-workers, professional colleagues, mentors, and in your own mind:

1. What are some of the benefits specific to your company you can accrue by implementing a sound communications strategy?

2. What lessons can you bring to bear to advance your C-suite's capabilities, whether they come from the White House briefing room, news footage, or your own experiences?

3. One way to engender C-suite support is to link your communications strategy to your overall business and public policy goals. How can you make that case in your business?

4. How can you nudge your company to think strategy before tactics?

5. Which specific professional development methods do your C-suite influencers prefer – colloquies with peers? Simulations? Skull sessions with an experienced consultant?

Bonus content

Long-term commitment is the hallmark of a sound communications strategy. Don't just take it from me. Go to www.barkscomm.com/APlusBonus and download your copy of "Why Your C-suite Improvement Plan Demands Long-term Focus," where you'll also profit from lessons by influencers like Warren Buffett, Jamie Dimon, and Daniel Pink.

CHAPTER 3

MEDIA RELATIONS

Once upon a time, newspapers published once a day and everyone gathered around the TV to get the day's news from Walter Cronkite. Communications and government relations executives could advise the C-suite how the day's news was going to play with some degree of certainty. Such was the daily news cycle.

CNN's arrival on the scene in the 1980s disrupted that pattern. That certainty began to erode thanks to the advent of the 24-hour news cycle. Now that arrangement has also been relegated to the dustbin of history, replaced by what I term the "Minute by Minute News Cycle." Stories that used to take days or weeks to unfold now take mere minutes. This includes everything from politics – witness the play-by-play aspects concerning the litany of White House woes – to cataclysms like hurricanes and plane crashes.

According to U.S. Secretary of Transportation Elaine Chao, "News-free existence is not a serious proposal, but it is worth noting that while today's 24/7 media environment is wonderful in many ways, it can also be like drinking out of a fire hose and intensify a downward reinforcing cycle of despair."

Under the current media regimen, every news organization competes with the others. Newspapers try to scoop the TV networks not for their print editions, but for their web content. And, of course, print editions of newspapers now face sibling rivalry from their own websites.

The accessibility of much of today's information via digital media outlets like Facebook and Twitter represents one of the main generators of the

Minute by Minute News Cycle. With a few touches on their tablets, reporters can access boatloads of data instantaneously – the same data that not so long ago someone would have had to sift through, copy, and mail to him, taking days or weeks. That assumes that they actually managed to connect following an unending swapping of telephone messages written on those once-ubiquitous pink message slips.

In the recent past, newspaper morgues served as an official record. It could take quite a while to unearth pertinent information by digging through musty old print editions or microfilm copies. Today we take for granted the ability to enter a search term on a website that reveals an often overwhelming compendium of facts and figures.

Drinking from a Fire Hose

Not only does information come faster in the Minute by Minute News Cycle, it comes in much greater volume. Think about it. How closely can you really follow any single individual or organization on the fire hose known as Twitter?

Your C-suite craves predictability. I understand. The fact remains it's harder today than ever before to provide that, and we are unlikely to move the needle back in the other direction. All this suggests a couple of revised strategies for dealing with the press.

Number one, when presenting positive news, it is to your benefit to cull the data and highlight the most relevant information so as not to overload the reporter. Sure, feature it on your digital media channels. At the same time, don't neglect more traditional outlets like your executives' speeches, your contacts with public officials, and, yes, even phone calls to key reporters who cover your beat.

Number two, if you are trying to get ahead of some bad news, the Friday evening "data dump," where you provide everything including the kitchen sink to get the story out all at once, may be in order. Just remember that you don't necessarily hold all the cards these days. News websites and digital media sources may dilute your ability to maintain control of the story.

Blogs also play a role in the Minute by Minute News Cycle. You should use them to your advantage whenever possible. Businesses that fail to monitor chatter on popular, reputable blogs are sure losers. Once a false story starts spreading, it's harder than wildfire to knock down in this day and age.

What does the Minute by Minute News Cycle mean to you and those senior executives you counsel? It means added vigilance in the form of razor sharp and consistent messages that you need to fine tune more frequently than in times past. Revisiting your messaging weekly during a crisis may have been sufficient previously. Now you would be well advised to reassess them far more frequently.

It also means that, more than ever, you must make an effort to grasp how you can facilitate the reporter's job. Some cranky media training participants tell me they don't think that's part of their job. Wrong.

Successful organizations understand that news gatherers are being forced to do more with less. The combination of public mistrust, layoffs, and budget cuts have made reporting as hard as ever. Buyouts of veteran reporters and the need for the remaining reporters to take on added duties affect your ability to reach out and touch the media. I've seen firsthand in our nation's capital the effect of office closures on regional reporters. The lucky ones are instructed to work from home. Others are out of a job. The greater your understanding of these newsroom facts of life, the greater the likelihood your good news will appear in print, online, and on the airwaves.

It is true that some news outlets don't train their reporters very well, for training is often the first place publishers look to cut. They rely on journalism schools to do the heavy lifting. That type of education is fine, but there is no substitute for real world experience. In many cases, particularly at smaller outlets, reporters can take advantage of ongoing education solely on their own time and on their own dime.

Yes, this makes your job as a news source more challenging. For instance, you may have to explain matters in greater depth to a cub reporter who lacks even the most basic understanding of your issues.

It's your job to explain these factors to your C-suite leadership. They may not want to hear it. Yet you have a responsibility to advise them appropriately. You should know your company and your leaders (and your own capabilities) well enough to realize whether you should take the velvet glove or the iron fist approach.

Consider how you can advance the goals of your organization by gaining a greater understanding of the challenges reporters face and, where appropriate, helping them rise to those challenges.

Respect for Reporters: Why It Benefits You

I often ask a series of questions when beginning to work with clients on their media strategy. One such inquiry is, "What is your opinion of reporters?"

I find it particularly helpful in smoking out preconceived biases that can get in the way of successful transactions with the media. This allows us to adjust attitudes during our work together. It's no secret that many spokespeople harbor antagonism toward reporters. I strongly advise you not to let that show.

Responses are all over the map. Many respond positively, indicating that most try to get to the truth and know their jobs. Others come back with words like skeptical and tough. Others evoke darker thoughts – sneaky, deceptive, rude.

As award-winning broadcast correspondent Christiane Amanpour says, "I believe that good journalism, good television, can make our world a better place."

It's not easy being a journalist. During my days as a reporter, I always appreciated sources who made my job easier. I served in that capacity long enough to know that there are all types of sources – the friendly and the combative; the hard-nosed and the hard to get along with. Yet this variety of personalities holds true in all walks of life. For example, just because a group of scurrilous accountants cooked the books in the Enron scandal does not mean all accountants are underhanded.

A useful perspective involves a primer on what a reporter's day is like. Today's reporters are under ever growing pressure to report on and write about multiple stories in any given day. After all, it's not like the old days when they had one deadline every evening. Now they must post content to the web and keep it fresh as new developments occur.

Their challenges range from incredible deadline pressures to gruff editors to poor sources. There may not be much you can do about the first two factors. The third, however, rests in your hands.

Respect for reporters is a must if you want to achieve success in print (be it hard copy or online), audio, and video. If your world view sees all journalists as slovenly and slipshod, they are likely to pick up on that and, consciously or not, paint the story about you in a less favorable light. That sound you hear is the success of your communications strategy swirling down the drain.

If, on the other hand, you enter into your media interviews with little in the way of preconceived bias, you're more liable to get a fair shake. It's human nature, and I have yet to find a way of overcoming that. Here's how I put it in perspective: The reporter wants a good story; you have a good story to tell. What a perfect match.

I've gotten to know many reporters over the years, both professionally and as friends. Some are open about the techniques they use to pry information from sources; others are more guarded. Some play buddy-buddy in an effort to get you to spill the beans; others come across as tough. Some will go off the record when the situation is right; others eschew that practice.

It is important to enter into a media interview with as few precon-ceived notions as possible while still conducting your background research on the reporter. It serves you well to determine such factors as how much they know about your issue, who else they have talked with, and what their interview tactics may be.

They are under constant deadline pressure. They need to get the scoop over the competition. It's not the easiest way to make a living, though it is professionally rewarding at times (and, yes, it is cool to see your name on a byline or to hear your voice on the air).

You'll get no argument from me that there are both bad and good re-porters. As in any vocation, you need to take the lazy with the proficient.

There are plenty of reporters who undertake a basic search for truth in their everyday work. They do not always report from the world's hot spots. Consider the scribe who covers your beat for a trade publication. Is she pesky? Does she ask lots of nosy questions? Does she insist on talking to your CEO when hot issues arise? Try to keep in mind, that's her job. The better the story you can feed her – on your terms – the better your long-term relationship with her and her publication.

What about the greenhorn reporter who works for your local newspa-per? Does he sometimes get under your skin when he tries to gain a better understanding of your issues? Is he constantly asking for background doc-uments? Be patient. He's learning what it takes to become a pro.

Ask your C-suite inhabitants, "What is your opinion of reporters?" If you hear a negative reply, you may want to work on an attitude adjustment. It'll be good for your company's communications strategy.

Ethics in Media: TV Anchor Suspended

Active reporters should not undertake a public affairs or communications role. Never. Ever. Similarly, communications consultants should not pre-tend to be journalists. Yet as the *Toronto Star* writes ("Global TV anchor Leslie Roberts suspended," January 8, 2015), one Canadian anchor recently tried to get away with this unseemly melding of roles.

There is so much wrong here, it's hard to know where to begin. To be sure, the case at hand is an in-your-face type of ethical transgression that merits an ashes and sackcloth punishment.

It is important to acknowledge, however, that less astonishing yet equally unethical transgressions go on regularly with individuals who try to straddle both sides of the journalism/communications fence. You can't be both a reporter and a communications consultant. It is a very bright line. If, for example, one claims to be a freelance reporter, one cannot accept pro-ject assignments from corporate clients. What happens when, in the course of your communications work, you deal with a confidential matter or hear about a juicy bit of news? Where does your ethical obligation rest if you also claim journalist status? There is no gray area. Really, there's just not.

The number of individuals who claim journalist status while also writing speeches, blog posts, etc., for the corporate C-suite – and do so with a straight face – astounds me. Anecdotally, I can testify that there is plenty of this going on. I understand the need to put food on the table and shoes on the baby. I suppose there comes a time when one is desperate enough to compromise ethical principles to feed one's family. Just please don't look me in the eye and try to convince me this is above board.

For you and your C-suite, this calls for an extra dose of due diligence when contacted by unfamiliar reporters. You owe it to your company to ensure that you are dealing with bona fide journalists, not hobbyists.

As one who has had feet firmly planted on the communicator side of the fence for 25+ years, I'm curious how (and if) journalists can help me understand this ethical rationalization for playing both sides of the fence. Seriously. How do you explain away such behavior?

Another Chapter in "What's Journalism? What's Not?"

The American Press Institute released in August 2015 results gleaned from a survey of more than 10,000 individuals with degrees in either communications or journalism.

Some of the results don't seem all that surprising. For instance, far more respondents believe the quality of the news they receive is declining. And I am heartened by the fact that, according to the findings, most don't think much of "sponsored content" (we called these advertorials in the not-so-long-ago). This tactic, sometimes called "native advertising," is a dangerous, borderline unethical trend designed to blur lines between real journalism and faux journalism.

One finding from the "What are these people thinking" department: Quoting from the study, "Fully 17% of these graduates who are employed by commercial brands consider their work journalism, as do 19% of those in politics, government and think tanks, 34% of those who describe themselves as entrepreneurs and 20% of those who work for technology companies."

Oh, please. If you work for a "commercial brand" (known in our non-jargon real world as a company), you are not practicing journalism. The same applies if you work in politics, at a think tank, or as an entrepreneur. You may offer valuable opinions or insights, but by no stretch of the imagination are you engaged in journalism. I'll admit that there are some increasingly blurry lines with respect to what is, and is not, journalism. Churning out copy for a private firm is nowhere near that line.

Here's hoping your C-suite does not think of your business as a journalistic organization. If they do, you have some educating to do.

Who Gets a Press Pass?

Who qualifies as a journalist? That line becomes more blurry by the day as freelance reporters and bloggers take on roles once reserved for traditional correspondents at well-recognized news outlets.

Not long ago, outlets like the Drudge Report and the Huffington Post were viewed skeptically by the mainline media. They now seem to have helped create a new mainstream.

One traditional standard measurement has been the media credential or, less formally, the press pass. Your company may not be in the business of deciding who's a reporter and who's not, at least on an official basis. Still, some organizations may find it helpful to rely on credentials from such bodies as the Congressional press galleries, federal agencies, and local police departments when they organize their media lists and decide who gains entrée into their news conferences.

In an effort to determine who merits credentialing, two Harvard outfits – the Shorenstein Center on Media, Politics and Public Policy; and the Berkman Klein Center for Internet & Society – issued a 2014 report titled, "Who Gets a Press Pass? Media Credentialing Practices in the United States."

Not all that long ago, it was pretty clear who received those passes that offered access to the Congressional press galleries and beyond the police tape. Do you work for *The New York Times*? You're in. A local television news department? Fine. A venerable trade publication? You bet. However, today's media world is not so black and white (may my newspaper friends forgive the pun). The Harvard study comments upon the conundrum and provides a clear picture of the current state of affairs. It is, sadly, short on suggestions for improvement. That may be due to the nettlesome nature of the problem.

You are likely in the market for practical solutions, not theory, so here are some suggestions that your organization may find helpful as you seek to clarify who qualifies as a reporter when it comes to your issues (in the interest of clarity, these ideas are mine, not Harvard's):

- Works full-time for a bona fide news outlet.
- Credentialed by a federal, state, or local government body.

- Claims experience as a freelance reporter and has recent clips to back up that assertion.
- Performs no work on the other side of the fence as a public affairs or communications consultant (a clear conflict of interest that could land your organization in hot water).
- Is not affiliated with an advocacy group, which could shade their coverage.
- Does not try to trick you with a bogus press pass they bought from a fly-by-night outfit.

You may opt to use one or more of these qualifications when making your decisions. There is no single right answer. This dilemma is not going to get any easier to solve in the years ahead. The continuing downward spiral of traditional media combined with the proliferation of independent outlets (some legitimate news sources, others mere personal mouthpieces) is likely to endure. All of which means that your decisions on who gets to cover your organization's news are likely to get even stickier.

This is a good time to discuss media objectivity. Smart and honest reporters and news sources acknowledge that there truly is no such thing. We all come at life and work with the baggage of our personal perspectives in tow. While ethical journalists strive to be objective, it has long been my contention that we would all be better served if we spread our cards on the table. His political philosophy, for example, may be left of center or to the right. He may personally agree with your message or vehemently disagree. We all have built-in biases. Being up front about them will lead to more fruitful and above-board interviews.

Gonzo journalist Hunter S. Thompson put it this way: "With the possible exception of things like box scores, race results, and stock market tabulations, there is no such thing as Objective Journalism. The phrase itself is a pompous contradiction in terms."

What does this mean for you? Fold this aspect into your pre-interview research. Get a sense of the reporter's take on your issue. Read or watch clips from her portfolio. Survey colleagues who have dealt with her before. Probe gently as you arrange the interview. The more you learn, the better you can couch your message in terms that may hit home.

Next, a look at some techniques to help your C-suite manage their exchanges with members of the media.

But I Repeat Myself

Repeat after me: Repetition is a good thing when dealing with reporters.

The question often arises during a media training workshop: If I have stated my message once, isn't that enough? Shouldn't the reporter get it the first time? In an ideal world, yes. But during my days as a radio reporter, among the news sources I appreciated most were those who reiterated their message numerous times throughout an interview. After the third or fourth time, it finally started sinking through my thick skull.

I am not talking about a robotic regurgitation. Use different words, examples, and proof points. Just make sure the main theme resonates throughout the entire interview.

Reporters are a busy lot, more so these days with newsroom cutbacks the order of the day. They may be working on several wholly unrelated stories at one time. They may be thinking about that spat this morning with their editor or news director. They may be thinking of what they need to pick up at the grocery store on the way home tonight.

The easier you make it for them, the better the chances your company's story appears in print or on the air in a way that is positive for your C-suite and your business. While there are no guarantees that your word gets through unfettered, reinforcing that message time and again is smart strategy.

Tried and True Techniques

Logistics matter. You need to consider so many minute specifics when offering up your C-suite to the media. You, not they, are the expert in media relations and how to relate to reporters, so explain to them what it takes to become a media influencer. Let's cover some of the particulars.

To the extent possible, control the setting of your interviews. Granted, if the interview takes place in a TV studio, you are not likely to have much flexibility. If a camera crew comes to you, scope out the background very carefully. Make sure, for example, that there are no charts on the wall giving away confidential information. If your COO has written a book, its cover could make a nice inclusion as part of the backdrop.

You can and should use some forethought in choosing the interview site even when video is not involved. Is your CEO's office the best place? Perhaps a conference room in your office suite? If reporters seek you out at a big offsite convention, is there a room you can duck into to gain some privacy?

When a telephone interview is the order of the day, determine how they operate at peak performance. Do they prefer to sit or to stand and wander? I try to nudge my clients to stand since breathing is easier, but if that makes them too uncomfortable, sitting can work providing they don't slouch and collapse their breathing and energy level. Do they have a reliable speaker phone or headset so they can keep their hands free to jot down ideas and reference the messaging notes you've prepared for them?

Also impress upon your C-suite the wisdom of setting – and enforcing – time limits on their interviews. Your communications shop will want to make this agreement with the reporter when arranging the session. Tell your C-suite about the timing so they know the game. In my experience, going much longer than 20 minutes allows time for one thing: Giving your spokesperson sufficient time to insert foot in mouth. Be on the alert for reporters who try to play buddy-buddy with your leadership. You've probably heard something like this: "Gee, we're having such a nice chat. How about just another quick five minutes?" Thirty minutes later, your exhausted C-suiter is casting the evil eye at you for all those "quick" questions that made him squirm to no end. One added factor about time limits: Never permit your leadership to play the heavy by noting the time limit and calling a halt to the proceedings. That's a communications pro's job. Your C-suite should be kept above the fray.

Satellite Media Interview Strategies

The time may come when you accompany your C-suite influencers as they sit in an often cramped studio and talk to a series of TV news anchors in far-flung cities via satellite. This is known as a satellite media tour (SMT). When participating in this type of interview, tell your executives to maintain eye contact with the camera; the lens becomes, in effect, the reporter in that distant city. This is one of the very few times it is permissible to look straight into the camera.

Your interviewee will be using an earpiece (known as an IFB) to hear the questions. If the earpiece falls out mid-interview, it's okay to replace it as best as possible. A floor manager may come to their aid when they are off camera, but don't count on it. This is not a format most people utilize on an everyday basis, so practice technique diligently during your media training session.

Hydrate by drinking lots of water the day before the SMT. These interviews are both mentally and physically taxing, so keep a glass of water handy for your executives during the shoot, too.

Advise your C-suiter to focus on your message, and to let the technicians deal with all the equipment. To help along those lines, write out the name of the reporter they are talking to, along with the city and station, and keep it in plain sight.

Use anecdotes and examples that are appropriate to the respective cities. Keep messages short and succinct; these are quick-hitters, so there's no time to emphasize more than two or three high-level points.

SMTs typically take place early in the morning to hit morning drive newscasts at stations across the country. They tend to be marathon sessions with many interviews in rapid succession packed into three or four hours. Be sure to schedule a good night's sleep the night before. Also, consider an afternoon nap the previous day. Oh, don't forget to smile or nod when being introduced, provided the interviews don't center on a solemn topic.

Skype Interview Etiquette

Even the highest profile media outlets have taken to holding interviews via online video services such as Skype rather than splurging for an SMT. Skype's quality isn't the best, but from the broadcasters' point of view, it is far cheaper than renting a studio for your appearance. Plus, it offers flexibility of delivering news from more remote locales. The Skype phenomenon means a new ballgame for news sources asked to participate in this type of remote exchange. While there are similarities between Skype and satellite media interviews, new twists exist, too.

For example, your spokespeople need to practice – a lot. Skype's newness on the news interview scene means that even long-time media sources have relatively little experience here. This mandates a few more simulated interviews before you undertake the real thing.

Be sure to look into the camera of the PC or mobile device. Some Skype interviewees tend to look at their monitor instead of the camera. Know where your camera lens is, and keep your eye contact locked there. Pay attention to your camera angle. Aim for a straight-on shot since viewers will not be enchanted by a view up your nose. Also, assume you are always on camera. You will likely have no way of knowing what is being broadcast at the moment, so avoid any embarrassing acts (yawning, scratching, cleaning your teeth, or worse).

Stage your backdrop. Something with your company logo or product or a book authored by your C-suite is fine, for example. On a related note, heed your lighting. Be sure you are adequately lit from a source in front of you. This allows you to be seen on TV and avoids plaguing your viewers with background glare.

Keep the background noise down, and use a microphone other than the tinny sounding one on your PC or mobile device. Finally, prepare for conversational delays. Connections are not always rock solid, so realize that you may have to wait a beat or two before hearing the next question.

Nine News Conference Niceties

The interview format with perhaps the highest pressure potential for your C-suite is the news conference. These often revolve around high stakes issues. Organizing a news conference requires flawless orchestration, so use these techniques as a guide for success during your next press briefing:

1. **Choose your spokespeople wisely.** Maybe it's your CEO, maybe not. And might you need additional experts to deal with technical issues?

2. **Hammer out your magnetic message.** It must be airtight, succinct, and easy to recall if you have hopes of surviving rigorous media scrutiny.

3. **Organize a media training workshop to deal specifically with your upcoming news conference.** Decide whether you have the expertise to handle this internally or need a consultant dedicated to media training.

4. **Make the rehearsal as authentic as possible.** Bring in cameras and light kits, and a handful of co-workers to portray reporters.

5. **Fire questions at your spokespeople during your media training workshop.** Sprinkle in some expected questions and some real hardballs.

6. **School your spokespeople in Q&A techniques**, such as bridging, flagging, deflections, and sneak peeks.

7. **Make sure you have access to the room where your event will take place at least one hour ahead of time.** This gives you time to iron out any technical kinks, offers your spokespeople time to get acclimated, and allows for a dry run.

8. **Instruct your spokespeople on how to control the crowd.** They should be the ones to call upon questioners and bring the proceedings to a close.

9. **Spell out the ground rules for reporters in attendance.** You can lean on those rules for more effective control when needed.

How to Talk on Talk Radio and Podcasts

Experts from a wide range of fields are eagerly sought by radio and podcast producers. You don't need to be a best-selling author or world-renowned athlete. Business leaders, community volunteers, and local public officials are frequent guests.

I'm an old radio hand and love the medium. Yet I readily admit that it has suffered a steep decline in the past few decades. I blame three factors. First, consolidation of ownership has dealt a death blow to many local stations. That friendly DJ's patter you enjoy? He may be ensconced in a studio hundreds of miles away. Corporate ownership has sucked nearly all of the "local" out of local radio.

Second, the Federal Communications Commission did away with the Fairness Doctrine in 1987. This valuable element of public policy eliminated the requirement that radio stations devote time to news and public affairs.

Third, the advent of crude, brutish syndicated talk shows has given stations ready-made programming. Why produce local news and talk if they can buy it on the cheap?

Talk show host extraordinaire Regis Philbin set the model for how a host ought to act by saying, "When you're a co-host, you've got to consider what the other person is saying and take the next step and get the laugh or get to the end of the story. You've got to make it happen and then move on to the next story."

How do you go about securing an appearance if you are fortunate enough to find a good opportunity? In some cases, an interview will drop into your lap. But radio opportunities mainly occur when you take the initiative. Here is how you can secure an interview. First, target producers at stations that make sense for your issue, then follow up with a succinct pitch for an interview.

Give the producer your spokesperson's name, title, telephone number, and email address once the interview has been secured. Also, forward background information that tells your story, remembering to include a brief biographical sketch. Submit a list of sample questions for the host. You will be pleasantly surprised how frequently these are used.

Next, help to familiarize your C-suite interviewee with the host and the audience. You can do this by having them listen to the program beforehand. This is easier than ever nowadays since lots of radio stations stream their programming online and maintain archives for later listening. Ask where the recording of your program will be archived. Use this to conduct your post-interview assessment with your C-suite talker.

Produce a mock talk show in your office in which your "host" peppers the "guest" with tough questions. You ignore this preparation step at your own peril.

Finally, send a confirmation to the producer 24 to 48 hours before air time. Reiterate all pertinent facts such as the guest's name along with a pronouncer if necessary, and the date and time agreed upon.

Hello, Out There in Radio Land

As you prepare, give a lot of thought to your audience. Who are you trying to reach? Of course, your messaging reigns supreme. Draft a brief, focused message that you want your audience to remember. Once you have finalized it, jot down a few notes on an index card or two (card stock doesn't rustle and cause as much noise as paper) to bring with you to the studio. I also recommend writing out the call letters of the station and the name of your interviewer. Keep this information in front of you during the interview. In most cases, the radio host is your ally. He or she wants a solid interview just as much as you do.

Radio excels in motivating its listeners, so be sure to leave them with a call to action; same with podcasts. Make sure they know how to get in touch with you for more information. As the program ends, give them a website, phone number, or email address. You may be surprised how many listeners contact you to learn more.

A few words about technical difficulties: If something of a technical nature goes wrong, ignore it. It is the station's problem, not yours. Be of good cheer and patience, and hope the engineers solve the problem quickly.

And be prepared for a whirlwind of activity throughout the station: Staffers running, yelling, and evoking a state of general panic. Your job is to focus on performing during your interview and publicizing your intended message. After the interview, ask the producer and staff if they post the audio of the show online. You can use this to further promote your cause.

Talk radio and podcasts represent a great opportunity to broadcast your message to important audiences. Enjoy your experiences on the airwaves.

Your Media Rights and Responsibilities

In any interview format – be it radio, TV, or print – media sources have certain rights to which they are entitled during the "business deal" with a reporter. At the same time, there are responsibilities – standards to which sources must adhere when dealing with the media. Here's a checklist of those rights and responsibilities. It's a good idea to review these tenets with your C-suite, especially those members who don't participate in interviews regularly.

Your Rights

To know the subject of the interview and inquire as to what questions the reporter might ask.

- To set time limits in advance of the interview.
- To ask clarifying questions during the interview.
- To abide by the ground rules to which you and the reporter agreed.
- To ask who else the reporter is interviewing.

Your Responsibilities

- To be honest.
- To respond to reporters in a timely manner.
- To learn about the reporter and the media outlet for which she works.
- To say you don't know rather than guess at an answer.
- To maintain a sense of professionalism at all times.

Proven Methods Sure to Alienate a Reporter

Beyond those rights and responsibilities, there exists a catalog of expressions guaranteed to grate on any credible reporter. Should your C-suite speak any of these code words, they will bear responsibility for turning the interview into a negative experience.

- **"No comment."** Picture yourself waving a red cape in a bull ring. These two small yet inflammatory words will convince reporters that you have something to hide.
- **"Why are you asking that?"** It doesn't matter why they delve into a given issue. If the question is hostile or off-point, it is up to you to redirect the interview.
- **"The earliest I can get back to you is next week."** Rapid response to media inquiries separates the pros from the wannabes. Unless the reporter has indicated their deadline is, in fact, next week, reply quickly.
- **Take the long route to answer a short question.** Like the rest of us, reporters are crunched for time. Make your answers succinct; avoid a wandering tour of your issue.
- **"Our end-to-end solutions create functionality for enterprises using IT platforms across all vertical channels."** You might as well be speaking Martian. Use the Queen's English and leave the jargon back at the office.
- **"I'm not sure, but I would guess . . ."** You are now in the process of digging a hole straight to China. Don't speculate. If you don't know, say so, then move on to familiar territory.
- **"I can't tell you that."** You may not be able to discuss certain issues due to legal, personnel, or proprietary concerns. Reporters understand this, but you need to tell them why you cannot discuss a specific issue while remaining open to talking about other areas.
- **"You're not going to misquote me, are you?"** This is akin to asking your doctor if she prescribed the wrong medication. Ques-

tioning a journalist's professionalism is a sure way to get on their bad side.

- **"I don't have any background material on that."** Reporters are always seeking to flesh out their stories. They may not write about all the in-depth information you give them, but your materials can help put matters into context for them.
- **"It's the media's fault."** A desperate ploy and a refuge for scoundrels with something to hide.
- **"That's a dumb question."** There are few dumb questions if asked in earnest. But plenty of media sources come up with dumb answers.
- **"Tell me the name of your publication again."** If you don't know this one, you haven't done your homework and don't deserve to qualify as an expert news source.
- **"Call me back later; I'm too busy to talk to you now."** Don't sit by your phone waiting for that return call.
- **"You're just playing gotcha journalism."** If you can't stand the heat of Q&A, step out of the line of fire and let someone else do the job.
- **"I'm not the right person."** If you leave it at that, you have left the reporter hanging and missed an opportunity to get your company's story out. Always be sure to give them the name and contact information of the proper individual.
- **"But we bought advertising in your publication."** The polite term for this is "conflict of interest." Another good expression is "stupid." Buy an ad if you want. But don't expect coverage or preferential treatment as a result.
- **"I didn't realize you wanted an on-camera interview."** When a TV producer sets up an interview, always assume it will be on camera. Dress accordingly.
- **"I'd like to review a copy of your article before it is published."** You are not the editor. Standards of good journalism dictate that, at least in the United States, news outlets have the final say. That is as it should be in a society with a free press.

Spin Is a Sin

Another way to annoy reporters is to talk past their questions. You can witness this classic media relations transgression by watching the Sunday morning talk shows (Meet the Press et al.). This can be an exercise in frustration for all involved – the hosts, the guests, and the viewers. There are occasional bursts of honesty, yet the main style often seems to favor spin.

I'm not suggesting you need to blindly follow a reporter's off-point or hostile line of questioning. But there is an art to guiding the interview back onto turf you choose to tread upon. Part of that process involves acknowledging the reporter's question, then bridging to the message you are committed to delivering.

The bull in the china shop approach is for amateurs. They wind up looking like:

- A rude individual who doesn't give a darn about issues real people want to talk about.
- A greenhorn who has failed to learn basic communications strategy.
- A dunce who is incapable of mentally processing a simple question.

Spin is a sin. Your next media interview may not occur under the bright spotlight of the Sunday morning talkers. No matter. In any interview, you need to acknowledge every question and skillfully build that bridge to your desired message.

What Is Off the Record?

Things can get bumpy when sources claim to be misquoted. My view? This rarely occurs. When someone claims to be misquoted, it is normally little more than a scoundrel alert – someone who either lied and got caught or has no talent for dealing with the press.

Or they may have naively stumbled into another area ripe for misinterpretation. There can be disagreement – sometimes strong disagreement – about how and when media sources should conduct "off the record" interviews with reporters. Bona fide communications experts see the value in this technique; those with less insight say it should never be used (with some even going so far as to claim there is no such thing as off the record).

They might as well say the earth is flat. This stance means that 1) they have no idea what it truly means or how to use it and 2) they don't play in sandboxes big and sophisticated enough to understand its importance. Savvy media sources who live in the real world and play with high stakes issues understand the value of off the record.

In fact, the practice is very real, as evidenced by its long-standing tradition as part of the media relations toolkit. Those who ignore this reality are depriving themselves and their spokespeople and clients of a potentially valuable tool.

When you deem it wise to go off the record, "on background," or "not for attribution," follow these 10 recommendations:

1. Keep media interviews on the record unless there is a compelling reason to do otherwise.
2. Develop and adhere to recommended standard definitions of off the record and other media relations techniques.
3. Distribute those definitions to reporters, communications practitioners, and to professional organizations to which they belong in an effort to achieve greater consistency and to minimize misunderstanding.
4. Educate communicators, especially those with no media experience, on both the meaning and the value of conducting interviews off the record when warranted.
5. Enter into off the record arrangements only with trustworthy reporters.
6. Agree to ground rules before beginning an interview.
7. Ensure that both parties explicitly agree to abide by the ground rules.
8. Confirm that both parties are empowered by their organizations to enforce the confidentiality of off the record interviews.
9. Negotiate ground rules before every interview, even if simply renewing the conversation after a short break.
10. Refrain from using such canards as "there is no such thing as off the record" or "off the record is a lie."

One of the most perplexing facets of conducting interviews off the record is the lack of a consistent definition. Let's clear up that mystery right now:

- **On the record**: Anything a source says can be quoted and any information supplied can be used with no restrictions. Documents and nonverbal signals are also fair game. Unless there is a compelling reason forbidding it, on the record interviews are the safest way to proceed.
- **Off the record**: Nothing provided off the record can be used in print or broadcast. This is most frequently used to steer reporters in a particular direction while attempting to leave no fingerprints. Only experienced communications pros – preferably those with a journalistic background – should go off the record, and then only if they know and trust the reporter and media outlet.

- **On background**: The reporter can use freely any information a source provides, either orally or in writing. However, the reporter cannot quote the source either by name or by other identification. Going on background is useful for individuals who deal with the media but prefer that quotes come from others in the company.
- **Not for attribution**: The reporter may publish information provided by sources. In addition, the source can be quoted, though not by name. The reporter and communicator must negotiate how the source will be identified (e.g., a company vice president, a source familiar with the negotiations).

In the final analysis, the most straightforward way to proceed is to keep most interviews on the record. But when that is not feasible, adhering to the 10 recommendations listed above can guide both reporters and their communications counterparts to a deeper understanding and to a lessening of disagreement over the use of such techniques as off the record.

Reporters Are Overdosing on Off the Record

Some reporters and media outlets – especially high-profile publications like *The Washington Post* – make too much use of "off the record" comments.

Scan the front page and you'll see an untold number of quotes attributed to:

- "A senior administration official."
- "A source who attended the meeting."
- "A negotiator involved in the talks."

I don't mean to call out the *Post* exclusively. It's my newspaper of record, and a beacon of classy reportage. Indeed, its emphasis on inside-the-Beltway news probably represents much of the reason for the overuse; not leaving a trace behind has been raised to a high art in our nation's capital.

When used properly, off the record is a meaningful media relations device. Unfortunately, it has been transformed into an overused – and lazy – means of getting a story. It must be the exception, not the rule.

How has this come to pass? It seems to have coincided with the rise in the Minute by Minute News Cycle. Reporters, along with their editors and publishers, are now in a mad rush to be the first with a hot story. Big news goes directly to the website and to Twitter before going to print. I understand the competitive nature of today's news business. But solid, sourced journalism is suffering as a result of this off the record mania.

It is impossible to dismiss the competitive nature of this issue. News outlets want to get the story first. It's good for business and when applying for the cornucopia of awards that have sprung up. Yet journalists need to ask themselves the hard question: Is it worth it if you have to routinely use unnamed sources? Let's face it, a story has less impact if no one comes forward publicly to stamp it as true. Putting a name and a face to the narrative lends untold credibility.

What is the solution to this abuse? It's not an easy fix. Reporters must be persuaded and educated to do a better job of holding sources' feet to the fire and insisting they speak on the record. By no means am I suggesting a ban on the technique. There are times when off the record is appropriate: Think Pentagon Papers or White House scandals. But good journalists use it judiciously. And those who are overusing it should be instructed by editors and readers to lean on it less regularly. Remember, it's the exception, not the rule.

Journalism and communications schools also have a role to play. The next generation of reporters needs to learn when – and when not – to go off the record. It would also be wise to teach them the precise definitions so that we have a more common understanding in the media marketplace.

Five for the Future

You've taken in the advice from Chapter Three. Now is the time to implement the thoughts that can help your company. Use these "Five for the Future" discussion questions to help you sustain your C-suite's professional development over the long run. Discuss these issues with co-workers, professional colleagues, mentors, and in your own mind:

1. What type of snap exercises can you use to sharpen your C-suite's capabilities to deal with reporters and to help them grasp the intense deadline pressures newspeople deal with every day?
2. How often should you commit to holding informal Q&A sessions with your C-suite leadership? And how frequently do you need to schedule periodic media training workshops for all of your spokespeople?
3. Is your media relations team staffed by ex-reporters who know how journalists think and what they need? If not, how does this hinder your operations?
4. When is the last time you conducted an audit of your list of media contacts? How often should you review it?
5. What media outlets – traditional or digital – should you pay more attention to?

Bonus content

Are your C-suite influencers prepared when that reporter opens her notebook or the studio lights shine in their eyes? I have some extra pointers for you. Log on to www.barkscomm.com/APlusBonus for your copy of "Ten Techniques to Employ when the Media Glare Shines on You."

CHAPTER 4

PUBLIC SPEAKING

Every audience is different. Your C-suite influencers need to find a means of learning who is in the house and what they need to hear. For example, it's important to know how many are expected to attend; their degree of support, hostility, or ambivalence; an age and gender profile; and their level of expertise regarding your subject.

How to unearth this treasure trove? Everyone loves lists. You've no doubt seen articles replete with them – "Top 10 Tips to Take-out Food." "The Six Mysteries of Dryer Lint." "A Dirty Dozen House Cleaning Hints." Say what you will about the usefulness of some of these surveys. There is one list that is worth its weight in gold to any speaker – the attendance list.

You can more effectively reach their audience when you take time to learn who is in attendance and why they decided to attend. I am not talking about violating someone's privacy or delving into their deepest, darkest secrets. But public speakers need to know what makes audience members tick.

The most basic question: Who are they? Get that advance attendance list from the meeting's organizers to determine their general level of sophistication regarding your topic. For instance, I need to target my remarks differently if I see a roster replete with senior communications decision-makers versus one filled with public policy savants. The attendance list will also tell you if you can expect any familiar faces – either friendly or antagonistic – in the crowd. Bonus tip: Request a list when you first agree to a speaking engagement, then request regular updates; that list is bound to change right up until the moment you step on stage.

Next, find out how large a crowd is anticipated. Among other things, this will affect your room set up. With a larger audience, you may opt for theater style seating rather than a U-shaped table, for example. The size also tells you how much material you will need to distribute.

Another question many speakers ignore: What is the age profile of your audience? This not only gives you some indication of the seniority of those in the room. You will find that older listeners tend to have longer attention spans. Recent cultural shifts mean that younger crowds are more attuned to multiple inputs delivered in rapid fire. Having a sense of the age range helps you reach listeners by using their preferred style.

Getting to Know You

Do your best to learn whether audience members are already acquainted. If they are not, you might choose to give them a bit of time to break the ice with some interactive pursuits. If they are familiar with one another, are there any boss/employee relationships to consider? I also like to learn if attendance is obligatory. People who sign up of their own free will are generally a whole lot more pleasant and receptive than an office that was led on a forced march to your presentation.

Is your audience more heavily female or male? This is valuable knowledge for a couple of reasons, none of which have to do with eligible speakers finding a date for Saturday night. First, hecklers tend to be male. I am not suggesting that every audience contains a heckler. Far from it. But if your subject covers delicate ground, be aware that a heavily male audience raises the odds for interruptions. Also, female dominated gatherings tend to laugh more readily. While you may not be delivering a comedy monologue, the bonds of camaraderie may be stronger with a preponderance of women.

Assess your audience's level of knowledge as it relates to your talk. Are you teaching them new skills, which means you must proceed a bit more methodically? Or are they top experts in their field who are turning to you for specialized knowledge that is outside their area of expertise? In real-world terms, I approach an audience of newly minted college graduates experiencing their first job in a public affairs or medical education agency far different from a roomful of medical key opinion leaders who need to understand how to interpret complex scientific findings into everyday language.

Also consider your audience's point of view toward your remarks. They tend to fall into three broad categories:

- Hooray, you're my man!

- You're an idiot if you believe that!
- I can't wait to take a nap.

Clearly, you have some persuading to do if your audience research indicates your listeners populate either of the latter two classes.

Keep your eyes and ears open for a subset of the second group, the know-it-all. Maybe they hold an honest disagreement with your opinion, but maybe they bear a grudge because you got that coveted speaking slot instead of them. If you see one of these adversaries on the attendance list, be aware that they may try to hijack your talk during the Q&A session. Manage the questioning period accordingly.

Methods to Organize Your Presentations: The Pros and Cons

With your audience research in your pocket, it's time to choose how to structure your presentation. Don't let anyone tell you there is one proper method for every circumstance. The appropriate choice is what works best for your audience and what suits your style and comfort level. Let's talk about the advantages and disadvantages of each method:

- **Full text**

   PRO: All but impossible to go off message; affords a convenient handout.

   CON: It is a challenge to read a speech out loud while sounding natural. Be ready to commit to a great deal of rehearsal time.

- **Outline or talking points**

   PRO: Avoids the "canned" sound of a full text speech while keeping you on track.

   CON: Speakers sometimes lose their train of thought. It is more difficult to get that train chugging again when using this bare-bones tactic.

- **Presentation software, slides, or overhead transparencies**

   PRO: Allows you to demonstrate visual concepts.

   CON: Too often a slide show turns into a mind-numbing experience that lulls the audience to sleep.

- **Extemporaneous (remarks are prepared but not written out)**

   PRO: Useful if you speak about the same topic to the same type of audience frequently.

CON: Strong temptation to veer off into uncharted waters.

- **Impromptu**

  PRO: None. I vehemently discourage this "winging it" method.

  CON: You will lose your train of thought, fail to deliver your message, and look like an unprepared amateur.

- **Stump speech**

  PRO: Maintains your consistency of message while allowing you to tailor matters to your specific audience.

  CON: Since this is a variation of the full text speech, you must work hard not to sound canned.

How to Prepare Your Next Presentation

Let's dig into some of the moving parts to assemble as you prepare. The first consideration is to make a conscious decision whether you want to address the organization that invites you. Next, conduct some research into your audience. This type of digging is essential.

And by all means settle on your message before you begin to draft remarks. Then determine the format of your presentation: Full text speech? Outline? Notes? Extemporaneous? A note here: Never default to using slides every time; decide whether they are appropriate for the specific occasion.

With your message in hand, enliven your remarks with quotable quotes, using tactics like stories, numbers, case histories, third-party references, and current trends.

Pay special attention to your opening and close. Even noted chef Julia Child recognized this: "Drama is very important in life: You have to come on with a bang. You never want to go out with a whimper."

Of course, diligent practice is mandatory. Weave a review of notes and videos from past presentations with an eye toward improvement.

Request the room setup you want. Do you prefer classroom or theater seating? Need a projector and screen? What type of microphone? Maintain dialogue with the event organizer to stay abreast of any changes, and stay up to date with any last-minute developments regarding your subject. Be sure to confirm all logistics, such as date, time, site, and length of your remarks, and to obtain an emergency contact number for the day of your presentation in case you are delayed or an emergency arises.

But I Wanted the Lectern Over There

At last, you arrive at the site. Ah, now your preparations are complete, right? Well, not quite.

Don't give short shrift to the preparation needed once you arrive at your venue. Your idea of the perfect speaking environment and that of the crew that set up the room may paint two starkly different pictures.

You may have requested an overhead projector, flip chart, and microphone. But are they in the room? Of equal importance, does everything function flawlessly?

You also need to consider the seating chart. Perhaps you requested classroom style seating with tables only to find the tables missing. Or you requested theater style seating with the rows slightly angled (bonus hint: This allows every audience member to face you and avoid craning their necks, plus it allows you to squeeze in a few more chairs), yet you discover the rows run straight across. Setup snafus happen with even the most carefully crafted plans.

Have you checked out the audio to ensure there are no dead spots caused by blown speakers? Did you run a sound check to determine which "hot spots" might generate feedback from your microphone?

Safety First

As a presenter, you take on the role of leader. Part of this responsibility involves the well-being of your audience. If a fire alarm sounds, you are the one who must calmly guide them toward the exits. "The one permanent emotion of the inferior man is fear – fear of the unknown, the complex, the inexplicable. What he wants above everything else is safety," noted H. L. Mencken. This means, of course, you must know the way out. I sometimes get strange looks from hotel staff as I prowl the service corridors seeking the fire doors in preparation for a speech. I don't care. The security of my audience outweighs a few funny glances.

As you arrive an hour in advance of your scheduled start time, make friends with your audio/visual technician. He is your ally and can make you look and sound very good (or very bad). Give specific instructions. This is your show, so take charge (diplomatically, of course). Discern whether your crew knows the ropes. Some are accustomed to running audio and video equipment, for instance; others do so only rarely.

Also, familiarize yourself with your new environment. Get a sense of the room. Become comfortable with it. Remember, you are the owner of that space for the duration of your presentation. Sit in the seats before your audience arrives. Are there any obstructed views? What do you need to do to ensure everyone can see and hear you?

Complete your technical preparation before your audience begins to trickle in. As they arrive, shake some hands. Be accessible. This helps ease your mind, gets the audience on your side, and buys you a few friendly faces.

Baseball slugger Roger Maris said, "You hit home runs not by chance but by preparation." This also applies to public speaking. Flawless preparation provides you with the power to knock one out of the park during your next presentation.

Now let's take a quick-hitting look at advice to help smooth your road to speaking success.

Top 10 Opening Lines Guaranteed to Turn Off Your Audience

There's a lot of truth in the old adage, "You don't get a second chance to make a first impression." Accomplished public speakers know that they need to get the audience on their side the moment they step on stage. Here are some openers to avoid at all costs:

- **Open with a joke**. Few of us can tell jokes effectively. Why not begin with a surprising or seemingly contradictory statement as an alternative?
- **Say "Good morning" or "Good evening."** Your audience already knows what time of day it is.
- **Speak in a monotone**. You might as well hand out sleeping pills. Make sure your Audio Tools – the way you sound – are in good working order.
- **Recite a dry litany of facts**. You are better off grabbing audience members' ears with a personal anecdote or a provocative thought.
- **Begin with a long, convoluted story**. Start simple and expand during your presentation.
- **Come onstage with eyes averted and shoulders slouched**. Maximize your Video Tools – the way you look.
- **Ask a confusing question to which no one knows the answer**. Beginning with a question is fine. Just be sure its complexity does not distract your audience from your presentation.
- **Recite a ribald tale**. Bawdy language has no place in a professional environment.
- **Mention religion or politics**. Even if your audience is religious or political in nature, these topics are the third rails of public speaking.
- **Belittle the previous speaker**. Do unto others ...

Slide Show No-nos

Some speakers use slides to great effect; others have no clue, larding them up with dense bullet points. Some speakers are comfortable with the technology; others quake at the thought of managing a laptop. Here is a handy list of things to avoid when you make the conscious decision to use slides. Never:

- Assume you need to deliver a slide show every time. It makes sense in some situations, not in others.
- Believe that people come to see your slides; they come to see you.
- Show slides that are so dense or complex that your audience finds them incomprehensible.
- Talk to the screen; converse with your audience instead.
- Say "next slide please" if someone is advancing the slides for you.
- Travel without a backup of your slide show; if your computer dies, you can borrow someone else's.
- Forget Plan B. When something goes wrong, plot out in advance how you will continue with your talk.
- Darken the entire room, only the area near the screen.
- Use fonts that are too small to be viewed from the back of the room.
- Leave home without your remote control device that allows you to advance your slides without being tethered to the keyboard.
- Get carried away with animation and sound effects.
- Arrive without a hard copy of your slides; when the technical gremlins attack, this is your backup.
- Neglect to hold a technical run through in advance of your talk.

Taming the Teleprompter

When your C-suite holds forth in larger venues, they may decide to use a teleprompter to read their script. Whether it's their first speech using one or they are veterans of the technology, here are some points to bear in mind:

- Gain a comfort level with the equipment by doing lots of practice rounds.
- If you have not worked with a teleprompter before, be aware that you will be reading your text from one or more screens that appear transparent to your audience.
- Rehearse with the operator who will run the teleprompter during your speech to establish a rhythm that matches your rate and style.
- Provide your operator with your text well ahead of time.

- Make sure you can read the teleprompter screens. Know in advance whether you will need your glasses or a larger font.
- Rehearse with the actual equipment you will use during your speech. You can do this as the crew conducts light and sound checks.
- Notify your operator of any last-minute edits. Experienced operators can quickly and easily accommodate minor changes.
- Strive to sound conversational.
- Don't stress if you miss a few words. The crowd won't know.
- Remember to make the most of your nonverbal skills. Don't focus so much on the technology that you submerge your speaking strengths.
- If your teleprompter breaks down while you are speaking, have a hard copy of your remarks ready as a backup.

Top 12 Panel Moderator Methods

Senior executives from your C-suite are sometimes called upon to moderate panel discussions. Few, however, dedicate time to refining the skills required to successfully guide both panelist performance and audience Q&A. Here is a quick primer to put you on the path to becoming a master moderator:

1. Set expectations with event organizers by clarifying your role.
2. Collect concise bios from all panelists well in advance. You need a solid 30- to 60-second intro, not an exhaustive curriculum vitae recitation.
3. Do your homework. Gain familiarity with the issues and personalities.
4. Take the lead before the event begins by introducing your panel members to one another.
5. Start your panel promptly. This demonstrates respect for your audience. Remember, never punish those who arrive on time.
6. Inform your audience of the day's format right from the top. For instance, tell them who the panelists are, how long they will speak, and if you plan to entertain questions verbally or in writing.
7. Treat all panelists courteously. The moderator's job is to foster an enlightening discussion, not to take sides.
8. Involve all panelists in the discussion, as some tend to dominate, others to disappear.
9. Enforce agreed-upon time limits, both for the event and for each panelist's remarks. You may have to play the "heavy" at times.

10. Take charge during audience Q&A. Insist upon questions – no speeches. In rare cases, you may need to cut off rants from those with a personal agenda.

11. Come prepared with questions of your own in the event the audience is slow to get involved.

12. Handle disruptive audience members diplomatically yet firmly. If you anticipate trouble, appoint a "sergeant-at-arms" ahead of time charged with handling any flagrant offenders.

Avoiding the Afternoon Blahs

Whether you are serving as moderator, speaking on a panel, or flying solo, there are those times when all you're thinking about is a nice dinner with the family. Or a night on the town. Or your favorite easy chair and a good book.

But, no. It's someone else's turn to speak and you're stuck in a late afternoon meeting where the temperature in the conference room is cranked up like a Finnish sauna.

The presenter hands out hard copies of his slides as you enter. Then he walks to the front of the room, launching right into his pitch. He makes absolutely no attempt to capture your interest. Instead, he fires up his slide show, dims the lights, and begins to blather. In no time flat, you are in the Land of Nod.

This is not a positive development if you are the presenter. What can you do to ensure you don't play the role of human sleeping pill when it's your turn to speak? Fortunately, you have plenty of options.

Let us first consider that late afternoon meeting hour. To be sure, there are instances where you will be locked into a certain time slot. If, however, you are given a choice, I recommend you avoid the late afternoon hour as well as the presentation immediately after lunch. Our body clocks think of those as siesta hours.

Another factor to heed is the room environment. Assuring a comfortable room temperature (aim for slightly cool, but not bone-chilling cold) falls under the category of preparation. Introduce yourself to the facilities staff at the meeting site and make sure they are poised to move – and move fast – if you need to adjust anything, such as the thermostat. Write down their phone number on your speaker's notes so you can get in touch at a moment's notice should your room take on the feel of an oven or an igloo.

Now, about handing out your slides – don't do it. Audience members have less incentive to pay attention if they can read your thoughts in advance. Don't give them an excuse to check out mentally before you've even started (not to mention that you are the content; your slides are simply a supporting visual that lack context absent your words).

If you decide to utilize presentation software, consider doing so for only a portion of your talk. I tend to avoid slide shows immediately after a meal and during the late afternoon. It is an engraved invitation for an audience to become glassy-eyed. If you do opt for slides, turn down the lights near the screen and leave the audience bathed in light. This will minimize their snooze quotient.

Capture the crowd's interest early. Keep the focus on you. And maintain a comfortable environment. These strategies should help you keep your next less-than-prime-time presentation out of the doldrums.

Wearing Out Your Welcome

Rule number one for presenters: Never disrespect your audience. If you speak too long and overstay your welcome, you will be treated to the sight of fidgety audience members checking the time, thinking, "I hope this windbag wraps things up soon."

We all have jam-packed calendars. This includes the people in your audience. They may face a meeting with the boss, a conference call with a client, or a hot date for lunch. Regardless where they are headed next, their time is valuable. Respect it. This is all about their time, not yours, so use the good manners mom and dad instilled in you and end on time.

This forces many a speaker into tough decisions. There is only so much you can say in a limited time. Presenters often find themselves caught in a time crunch, desperate to cram in one last factoid or show all their slides.

You could no doubt speak for days on end about your area of expertise. But you don't have days. You may have 30 minutes or less. Thus, the challenge comes not in what you should include, but what you must leave out.

Here is how you can avoid this common presenter's trap.

First, time your practice sessions. If you are scheduled to speak for 30 minutes, aim for 20-25 minutes as you conduct your run throughs. Most of us tend to slow down when we speak in public. We also are likely to overestimate the number of words that can be jammed into a tight time frame.

Plus, you may be interrupted by any number of things, from audience questions to slamming doors. All those distractions eat up precious seconds. And, of course, the typical presentation tends to begin a few minutes late. Throw all these factors into the mix and before you know it, your 30-minute window has been chopped significantly.

You do not want pile more stress on your shoulders by forcing yourself to mentally edit as you speak. Moreover, the front of the room is a dangerous place to get creative. If you end a few minutes early, it is far easier to expand upon a point or stretch the time allotted to fielding questions from the audience.

Next, trim your talk to the essentials. I once led a presentation skills workshop for a group of renowned scientists, each of whom trooped in with separate sets of slides. The problem was they were presenting as a panel, leaving nowhere near enough time for individual slide shows.

As we practiced, it became clear their remarks would go way over the allotted time. One speaker, in fact, wanted to shoehorn 20 slides into 10 minutes. This had all the earmarks of a speechmaker's disaster.

To complicate the situation, a lot of the slides contained dense graphs and charts, making them hard to read and requiring in-depth explanation. Fortunately in this case, each of the scientists was an experienced speaker. After we discussed the dilemma, they were able to tweak their slide kits.

How did our team do when show time arrived? Thanks to their talents and the organization provided by the training, each performed magnificently, sticking to the agreed upon time limits.

The respect they demonstrated resulted in a happy audience hungry for more. Show your audience some consideration. They deserve it.

Top 10 Reasons Audiences Head for the Hills

Sad to say, some speakers fail to evidence that respect. They make for better sleep aids than a warm glass of milk. Others offend their audience and remain clueless. Don't let this happen with your C-suite. Here are some of the speaking sins that are sure to make an audience head for the exits, and deservedly so:

1. Punish those who arrive on time by beginning the program late.
2. Drone on in a monotone.
3. Leave the temperature in the room so stifling that audience members are fanning themselves and gasping for air.
4. Pose a question so esoteric that no one knows (or cares about) the answer.
5. Tell a story that rambles pointlessly before it eventually dies of boredom.
6. Talk to the slides instead of engaging the audience.
7. Attempt a joke that falls flat.
8. Insult the audience by insinuating that they are a bunch of stupid, unsophisticated rubes.
9. Mumble so that no one can possibly understand.

10. Ramble on past the allotted time.

Use an Evaluation Form, But . . .

Garbage in, garbage out.

To improve as a public speaker, you need solid information about your performance. Your audience's opinions form the foundation of the vital effort to assess feedback.

Some presenters never go farther than an evaluation form. While helpful, a piece of paper cannot tell you everything you need to know. Moreover, there are drawbacks to the evaluation form.

For instance, compliance is a real issue. Not everyone will fill one out despite your requests. In addition, you tend to hear from the extremes – the people who either loved you or hated you. Don't get me wrong. Evaluation forms can play a role in your improvement strategy. But speakers who hope to advance their agenda need more.

Fortunately, your tackle box contains plenty of added lures that can help you assess feedback. One basic option is to record yourself either via video or audio. If a professional videographer is on site, that's great. But in this instance, your sole interest is in assessing feedback. You don't need broadcast quality, so simply ask a friend or relative with a video camera to tag along and do the honors; they can even shoot the video on their phone. If video is not feasible, at least record the audio, using your mobile device or a digital voice recorder. Whatever you do, never let your recording gather dust. Watch or listen to it as soon as possible and critique yourself honestly.

Some clients in my presentation skills workshops look at me funny when I argue that their job is to communicate, not simply to present. What I mean by that is communication is a two-way street. You must be skilled both at sending and receiving.

Internalize to Verbalize

Grade A presenters live by this credo: Internalize to verbalize. In other words, gaining a comfort level with your remarks and practicing them sufficiently empowers you with a greater opportunity to process real-time feedback from your listeners. Such instantaneous audience feedback means observing the nonverbal signs your listeners send. Are they offering solid eye contact, smiling, and applauding? Is there a general sense of quiet in the room as you speak? All of these signals indicate you are hitting the mark.

There are also negative signs you must monitor. Are your listeners engaged in side conversations, reading newspapers, or checking texts and email on their devices? If so, you have some work to do to get them back in the corral.

An added word of advice: Keep your receptors open for clusters more than individual indicators. That guy on the aisle may be shifting in his seat because he has a bad back. The woman in the third row may have her arms crossed because the room is too cold for her. When I speak, I don't obsess about one or two negative signals. Your feedback is more accurate when you keep eyes and ears open for patterns.

Once you have concluded your remarks, your job is far from complete. Spend some time with audience members and ask them some pointed questions that may sound like this: What one or two items did you find most valuable? I sense the audience enjoyed the story about widget manufacturing; did you feel that, too? What will you do differently in your job based on what you heard today? One important note before you wade into the crowd: Prepare yourself for possible negative feedback. Never let yourself become one of those speakers whose face freezes uncomfortably upon hearing criticism. Receive such feedback with grace and a constructive attitude.

As soon as you depart your venue, write a few notes to yourself about the feedback you gained while the comments are still fresh in mind. A few days after your presentation, circle back with the organization that invited you to speak. Tell your contacts this is part of your ongoing effort to improve so you can be even better the next time you speak before them.

There is one point not to be lost when it comes to assessing feedback – gauging your own ability to critique your performance meaningfully. You may be a top-flight financial planner, IT programmer, or lawyer. But your expertise does not center on the art of public speaking. You need an expert set of eyes and ears – a trusted confidant – particularly if you are serious about sharpening your public speaking edge. Perhaps your next job, new client, or election victory hangs in the balance.

Five for the Future

You've got a better grasp of how to help your C-suite improve their public speaking abilities thanks to Chapter Four. How can you continue to enhance their influence? Use these "Five for the Future" discussion questions to help you sustain your C-suite's professional development over the long run. Discuss these issues with co-workers, professional colleagues, mentors, and in your own mind:

1. What types of speaking opportunities should you actively pursue for your C-suite?
2. Which of your executives is ready for a speech in that big auditorium? Which ones perform better in smaller venues?

3. Do you have a checklist to use when advancing the site for their presentations?

4. If you have an executive who defaults to using slides every time, how can you help him see the wisdom of using other formats, too?

5. Review your company's slide templates. Are they consistent and visual, or do they show a laundry list of boring bullet points?

Bonus content

Are you having trouble getting through to your C-suite when trying to help them enhance their presentation skills? You'll profit from the bonus advice when you log on to www.barkscomm.com/APlusBonus for your copy of "12 Roadblocks to Speaking Success – And How to Overcome Them."

CHAPTER 5

ADVOCACY

You have only so much public policy bandwidth, so choose your issues carefully. Leading the charge on your top concern is obviously a must. Unless you have massive resources and staffing capabilities, however, you may have to forfeit command of secondary matters. You have two options. First, simply put lesser issues on the back burner and get to them when they heat up or after you dispatch your primary focus. Second, let another organization take the lead and support its effort as best you can.

A clarifying note on the purpose of this discussion about advocacy. It does not involve lobbying. That is a distinct skill set that involves paying someone – either staff people or consultants – to actively pursue or block legislation on your behalf. My intent here is to deal with public affairs. For purposes of definition here, this encompasses experts who testify before Congress, state legislatures, local boards and councils, and regulatory bodies; and constituents who visit, write, or call their elected representatives.

Before we dig into specifics, some general advice: Be definitive in your dealings with policymakers when you make the all-important "ask" of them. For instance, getting friendlier legislation is not a goal. Stopping Congressional action on S.1 is.

When mapping out your advocacy plan, consider timing. Go where the grass is green. If, for instance, your state legislature isn't in session this year, it's useless to plan a maximum effort. On the federal level, if Congress is approaching election season or a holiday recess (I realize they are now officially called "district work periods," but really ...), hold off on that big push and perhaps devote your efforts to the regulatory side.

Also be sure to target the proper level of government. Visiting your member of Congress to discuss a local issue is a waste of time and reveals you to be an amateur. Likewise, approaching your city council when their hands are tied by state law is useless.

Effective Use of Your C-suite Officers

This is how a company should prepare its CEO to testify before Congress. The ingredients? 1) An eager and inquisitive CEO, 2) government relations and communications staffs that know how to team up effectively, and 3) a workshop to sharpen the executive's oral statement and performance at the witness table. At the conclusion of that workshop, he owned a five-minute statement that truly was five minutes (his first draft clocked in around seven minutes, risking the wrath of the committee chair), a firmer grasp of how to act while testifying, and an enhanced ability to deal with the tough questions anticipated from the members of Congress. The result? A successful appearance that advanced his public policy goals and delighted his staff.

Now, let's take a deeper look at a case study that serves as a model for your C-suite executives when they ascend to Capitol Hill.

Mark Zuckerberg Prepares to Walk the Plank

You may be a billionaire. You may have one of the most recognizable names on the face of the earth. You may have a stable of advisors. Congress will not be impressed.

Facebook CEO Mark Zuckerberg faced an immense set of challenges when he ventured to Capitol Hill in April 2018 to testify before a joint session of the Senate Commerce and Judiciary committees and in front of the House Energy and Commerce Committee.

You may well face similar hurdles, though are unlikely to attract the same level of attention as Zuckerberg. Some of his foremost challenges:

- He had never before testified on Capitol Hill. This is akin to asking a rookie to start the seventh game of the World Series. The prospects for victory, while not zero, are significantly diminished.
- He was unaccustomed to dealing with freewheeling Q&A. For example, he rarely indulges in media interviews and, when he does, likes a controlled situation. During a conference call with reporters the week prior to the hearing, Zuckerberg was reportedly more at ease than in the past. Still, dealing with reporters on the phone represents a more controlled situation than testifying before press-hungry politicians.

- His company was embroiled in a crisis that affects one billion daily users worldwide. Do you think that many people watching your performance might induce a bit of trepidation?
- The prodigy is not the most scintillating public speaker. He has a halting, unsure public persona. We can't all be born silver-tongued orators. Nonetheless, CEOs have a responsibility to communicate effectively.
- His arrogance leads him to think he's the smartest guy in the room. I'd wager that he was one of the least competent in that hearing room on the subject of politics and public affairs.
- It was interesting to watch how Zuckerberg handled the pressure. This is a tightrope walk for any first-time witness, especially before the often rough and tumble House Energy and Commerce Committee.

The stakes were high not only for Zuckerberg's personal reputation, but for the success of his company. Its stock price dropped significantly in weeks before his appearance, and a poor performance on the Hill could send it tumbling even further.

Ask Me Anything

Ostensibly, this Congressional hearing was established to review the Cambridge Analytica scandal during the 2016 U.S. elections, in which that company scooped the personal data of at least 87 million Facebook users. He needed to be prepared, however, to also face questioning from committee members antsy about other issues, including:

- Russian meddling in U.S. elections, and Facebook's allowance of fake accounts and fake political advertising.
- Privacy protections for Facebook users, and attendant potential investigations from the Federal Trade Commission and several state attorneys general as well as European regulators.
- Perceived political bias on Facebook's part.
- Whether the federal government should begin to regulate networks like Facebook, and what such a framework should look like.

One of the bigger questions: What would Zuckerberg's overarching message be? Would he come across as sorry? Defiant? Clueless? He had been sending mixed signals since the crisis sprang up. Initially, he took the habitual Facebook approach of hauling up the drawbridge and positioning the kettle of boiling oil. Remember, however, Zuckerberg's conference call with reporters during which he reportedly displayed a more open mea culpa style (while still proclaiming that he is the best person to run Facebook) and a simultaneous charm offensive in which the company trotted out Chief Operating Officer Sheryl Sandberg.

Never Aim for the Capillaries

In his oral statement and during Q&A, he needed to get right to the point. A tech-laden statement would breeze right over the heads of most members of Congress and of the public. And make no mistake, this was a public show as much as a Congressional hearing. His audience extended far beyond the four walls of the hearing room to Wall Street, Silicon Valley, and the living rooms of many Americans (ask yourself whether you had been tempted to delete your Facebook account in the wake of these ongoing issues).

Witnesses have limited time, and are always subject to interruption from members of Congress. My assumption is that Zuckerberg does not like to be interrupted, so would some committee members intentionally try to do so in attempts to rattle him? Reporters do it all the time. Lawmakers can play the game, too.

Q&A is where he would hit the jackpot or lose his shirt. Could members bait him into letting his arrogant side show and succeed at flustering him? His rehearsal sessions needed to include what I refer to as the Third Degree; herd your smartest and most skeptical people into the room and pepper the witness with the toughest questions imaginable. Nothing is out of bounds. Better to anticipate and frame answers to such queries in the security of your preparation efforts than to be blindsided on Capitol Hill. One indicator for the Facebook CEO: Would he have everyday examples to support his point of view, or devolve into tech talk?

Prepare for Battle

Zuckerberg had to take preparation seriously and shed the smartest guy persona. You can rest assured that he did not attend one of those relatively useless come-one, come-all general courses offered by some public affairs agencies or universities. He is not about to reveal his inner secrets or foibles in front of a roomful of strangers (nor should you, for that matter, when your time comes to testify).

He had to listen when his public affairs experts told him which members of Congress are for him and which are against him, for this offers some indication of where to anticipate the hardball questions (and some softballs perhaps). The CEO had somewhat of an advantage here since, in recent years, Facebook and other IT behemoths have ramped up extensive D.C. public affairs capabilities.

Then there was the issue of who wins the battle behind the scenes – the lawyers who typically want to reveal as little as possible or the communicators interested in broadcasting a Facebook-friendly message. This can be a real point of tension and, if left unchecked, can befuddle the poor witness left in the middle to try to sort things out for themselves.

The CEO couldn't wing it if he harbored hopes of exiting the hearing with his pride (and fortune) intact. Research shows us that practice is the single most useful step toward improvement. You can listen to experts all you want, but the path to improvement runs straight down Practice Boulevard. Judging from his few media appearances, the Facebook leader has yet to internalize many of the most basic communications strategies. If that trend held on Capitol Hill, he was in for a rough ride.

Staring Down Reputational Risk

Members of Congress will tear you apart if you come across as smug. That has financial and reputational consequences for Facebook. I'll leave it to business analysts with expertise in that area to judge what the fates may hold, both for Facebook and for Zuckerberg's career. If the face of Facebook has any doubts about possible consequences, all he needs to do is consult with Richard Smith, former CEO and chairman at Equifax, and John Stumpf, Wells Fargo's ex-CEO.

What You Can Learn from Mark Zuckerberg

They would tell him that testifying on Capitol Hill is no picnic. Testifying as a first-time witness is especially daunting. Testifying with the whole world watching is a real stomach-turner.

I'm not here to grade Zuckerberg's performance. Talking heads have ranked him all across the board. Rather, the goal here is to use his appearance to help you when your time comes – a look at the dos and don'ts.

Enter Stage Right

First impressions count for a lot, and Zuckerberg's day one entry looked tentative. He looked around the grand hearing room with a deer in the headlights look, seemingly asking himself, "Should I sit now?" He even appeared to ask one of his handlers if he should do so. Here's what to do: When you enter the room, head straight for the witness table with a purposeful stride. If members of the committee approach to shake your hand, fine, by all means be gracious and accept. To avoid that surprised gaze, get a glimpse of the hearing room ahead of time. If a personal visit isn't realistic, at least seek out some video to get a sense of its grand size.

Zuckerberg's nonverbal performance was better than I expected. He spoke with a strong volume, modulated his pitch, and generally maintained solid eye contact with panel members. Of prime importance, he nailed the five-minute time limit. He clearly practiced a lot and did a good job internalizing his remarks. This allowed him to appear more conversational than tightly scripted.

One item that has gone unnoticed in many quarters: When he said, "I'm sorry" for Facebook's lapses, his voice tightened and his pitch rose slightly. It's impossible to discern exactly what that means from this one indicator (beware those who claim an ability to read body language from a lone characteristic). What a signal like that tells me is that the issue is a candidate for further monitoring.

Sure enough, how many times did he repeat his apology during the Q&A? I didn't notice one instance. Perhaps he is not altogether comfortable apologizing. Maybe the advisors succeeded at putting it in his statement and he begrudgingly allowed it, then during Q&A he followed his own counsel and avoided apologizing. As a result, his oral statement and Q&A seemed not quite in sync.

Another subtle linguistic moment took place at the end of his oral statement. I was expecting the customary, "I look forward to your questions." Zuckerberg instead intoned, "I'm ready to take your questions." Not a big deal, but words matter. This sent a sly attitudinal signal to those paying close attention.

I'm Ready for Your Questions

On to the Q&A, where the Facebook CEO didn't make any truly embarrassing blunders (and really, weren't we all just waiting to see that, rather like those who watch the Indy 500 to see the crashes?). However, he proved less than adept at utilizing basic communications tools like bridging and flagging, which give the appearance of respect for the question and questioner. Instead, he clumsily dished out a response that either tried to sidestep or proved at best tangential to the query.

Zuckerberg let some uneasiness show when under questioning about Facebook's default settings and how they might affect user privacy. At one point, he shut his eyes briefly, essentially signaling, "Please don't hit me."

To his credit, for the most part he avoided talking over the lawmakers. At one point on day one he was tempted to try to drown out Sen. Ted Cruz (R-Tex.). Wisely, he thought better of it. There was more of this in the freewheeling House hearing, though Zuckerberg generally kept his cool. The one time it sneaked through was when Rep. Anna Eshoo (D-Calif.) hit him hard. Zuckerberg, with more than a hint of annoyance in his voice, insisted, "I'm answering your question."

Members of Congress will sometimes push you to answer with a simple yes or no. Avoid this trap whenever possible. Most issues of public policy are heavily nuanced; one-word answers fail to do them justice. Plus, you could put you and your company on the record as supporting or opposing something you had not intended to do. Be alert to the fact that, if you attempt to respond with a full sentence, you may be cut off. You just have to stand your ground and not play the yes or no game.

He never let his arrogance show to the point of overtly embarrassing his inquisitors, despite some truly stupid questions. He seemed puzzled by a thoroughly opaque query about 96 categories of something or other. Pausing for a moment, he began by saying, "Here's how I think of it," sparing Sen. Deb Fischer (R-Neb.) any more embarrassment than that which she caused herself.

If you detect a lack of sophistication, be prepared to provide some easy to understand examples. For instance, there was much talk of apps that use Facebook data. The legislators nodded knowingly, though I suspect many had no idea what this meant. Zuckerberg never gave any illustrations to enlighten them.

Pressed for Time

Most of the House members refused to let the witness offer extended answers due to the four-minute limit imposed on each of them. When you are under fire, the filibuster can prove useful. Granted, lawmakers know that trick, too, so you may not get away with it every time. But you can every now and then, as Zuckerberg found when Rep. Cathy McMorris Rodgers (R-Wash.) allowed him some longer form answers.

Witnesses need to remain alert for the quick, hard-hitting question. What to do when you need a moment to think through your response? Stall by using a throwaway phrase. Some examples:
- "Here's how we approach that issue ... "
- "That's a question I often hear. How do we deal with it?"
- "We've confronted that issue and here's what we've found ... "
- "Let me explain it this way ... "

Have a number of these phrases at the ready. If you issue the same wording every time, it will soon become evident that you are invoking a stall tactic. Also, avoid replying with, "That's a great question" or "I'm glad you asked that." In the first instance, it might make your questioners wonder if all their other questions are poor. Second, if you are stalling for time, it is pretty clear that you are in no way happy to hear that question. By the way, these techniques work equally well in media interviews.

You can play that game as the responder, too. Two examples from the Senate hearing come to mind. In response to an inquiry from Sen. Bill Nelson (D-Fla.), Zuckerberg offered a very short answer. Nelson was unprepared to issue his next question so soon. Second, when Sen. Orrin Hatch (R-Utah) appeared confused about how Facebook generates income, the CEO replied with a brief, "We sell ads," bringing the Utah solon up short.

It's moments like these that can help you exert a small measure of control. Never, however, labor under the impression that you can take charge. The chair has the gavel, committee members have the floor, and you are in the witness chair at their pleasure. That said, look for those rare times when you can be the leader. Zuckerberg did this when committee Co-chair John Thune (R-S.D.) tentatively called for a break, noting the witness would probably appreciate one. Zuckerberg spoke right up, saying let's go for "another 15 minutes," and got his wish. A small moment, to be sure, but one that signals a confident witness.

One verbal trick that Zuckerberg used drove me nuts for the entire two days. When launching into his replies, in nearly every instance he began with, "Congressman" or "Senator." My suspicion is someone in his phalanx of advisors told him to do this because it sounds respectful. That's true, and can work to your advantage. Overuse of the honorific in nearly every response, however, made him sound mechanical and over-rehearsed.

Can I Get Back to You?

There were numerous times he did not have information at his fingertips; that's fine when not overdone. If you try that too much, it fails the laugh test. Zuckerberg overused that trick during the first day's Senate hearing (it's hard to believe he knew nothing about cross-device tracking, for instance). He kept telling committee members that his "team" would furnish the details. That's not good enough. The fact is members of Congress want your commitment of personal responsibility as the main player. Sure, to a degree this is just linguistics. But, again, words matter.

Public officials expect to see your CEO, so if you hope to make strides with your public policy objectives, get the big guy involved. Should communications staff play a role? Yes, although remaining in the background to take notes and to diplomatically prompt the boss if they forget to raise a key point.

Make sure you review likely questions during your preparation phase. In Facebook's case, one clear and longstanding point of weakness is the lack of diversity in the IT field. Zuckerberg needs a ready response to this, yet surprisingly failed to have one handy. He should know enough to out-line specific steps. And why he failed to agree to an IT CEO summit as suggested by Rep. G.K. Butterfield (D-N.C.) is baffling; it's such an easy concession.

One of the biggest faux pas took place not during his testimony per se, but during a break in the proceedings. When he got up to exit the room, he left his notes on the witness table. Big mistake. One of his handlers should have noticed this and been charged with picking them up and guarding them. His advisors failed him miserably on this count.

On the subject of your staff, make sure they watch their conduct. Zuckerberg's "body man" – the fellow sitting directly behind him in the camera shot – had one of the hardest jobs of anyone: Looking interested for five hours straight, two days in a row. To his advisors' credit, I spotted only one major breakdown. When their charge was caught trying to finesse a response about a terms of service violation associated with a Federal Trade Commission consent decree, both staffers visible on camera went right to their mobile devices, presumably texting colleagues for more back-ground or to indicate to their press people that they might expect questions on the subject. You can bet that Sen. Richard Blumenthal (D-Conn.) knew he hit a nerve when that texting flurry took place.

Zuckerberg did reinforce key points along the way – the need for bet-ter artificial intelligence tools to detect bad actors, and successes in rooting them out in recent elections in Alabama and globally. Such repetition is a good thing, for committee members often come and go in the course of a hearing.

Running on a Full Tank

Interestingly, he seemed to gain energy as the first day's hearing progressed. Maybe he was getting more comfortable in his surroundings. Maybe he started to think this testimony stuff wasn't so hard after all. Maybe he gains an extra burst of energy late in the afternoon. It led me to wonder if he had tapped all his reserves and whether he would be left with an empty tank for the next day's House inquisition. After all, two high profile Congressional bouts within 24 hours would test the mettle of even an experienced witness, which Zuckerberg was not. His energy level looked fine to begin on Wednesday, though it did flag later as demonstrated by his switch to orange juice from water. He likely felt the need for an energy burst. His syntax also started deteriorating as the afternoon wore on. The lesson for you is to pay attention to your energy level. If, for instance, you tend to be a night owl yet are summoned to testify in the morning, realize that you may not be at peak performance and adjust your practice schedule and sleeping habits accordingly.

The style of the two hearings varied quite a bit, and Zuckerberg seemed somewhat taken aback by the punchier House style. The signs were evident early on when, in his opening statement, ranking minority member Frank Pallone (D-N.J.) served up some anti-Republican words. Zuckerberg was smart enough to avoid that game. If two other parties are going at it, sit back and let them tear each other apart.

There are a couple of factors at play here. Senators are accustomed to treating us to windier speeches. They can go on for eons on the Senate floor while House members must adhere to tight time limits.

It's important to understand who your questioners are. This needs to be a vital part of your preparations. For example, there are times when you can take a mini-break when under questioning from those inclined to offer a three-minute speech (looking at you, Sen. Hatch). Then there are the members who want to smack you right upside the head and try to throw you off balance with a quick pinprick question (hello, Sen. Maria Cantwell (D-Wash.)).

In addition, members of the House are able to concentrate on their issues more closely. There are 435 of them and only 100 senators, so the law of numbers dictates that the Senate side is spread more thin. What does this mean to you? Questioning on the House side tends to be more informed, and that was evident during Zuckerberg's hearing. Sure, there are stars and duds on both sides of the Capitol. Generally, however, the House is more detail oriented.

I was also curious during day two whether the CEO would try to humanize himself with a few more smiles and (seemingly) off-the-cuff bon mots. That didn't happen, maybe for the better. That is not who Mark Zuckerberg is, at least as far as his public persona is concerned (hey, for all we know, in private he may be the guy at the party with the lampshade on his head). Playing to strengths is important, and if he is not comfortable playing buddy-buddy with members of Congress, no sense in forcing it.

Beware the Trap Door

The one time he did smile before the Senate committees was when Sen. Richard J. Durbin (D-Ill.) began by asking Zuckerberg if he would be comfortable telling senators what hotel he stayed in last night and who he had texted with recently. After a few seconds of squirming, the CEO flashed an uncomfortable smile and demurred. Durbin's point? Facebook may know which hotels its users frequent and who they text, but Zuckerberg wanted to maintain his privacy.

When the curtain closes on your hearing, exit with grace. Do not do what Zuckerberg did when handed a copy of the constitution by one House member. The CEO barely looked at it, then handed it off to an aide. Bad form.

Shake hands with committee members and take time for an informal word or two. I advised the president of one organization who was raked over the coals by one of Congress' grand inquisitors. They had a most collegial chat afterward. No, they didn't agree, but it did open the door to a less hostile relationship down the road.

The Seven Deadly Signs: When You Need Testimony Training

No question about it – as Mark Zuckerberg no doubt experienced – testifying before Congress or your state legislature is a daunting challenge that requires maximum preparation.

Those who persuade lawmakers to accept their point of view work hard to do so. Experience and expertise at the "legislative dance" is crucial, as is planning and preparation. Moreover, development and effective use of your company's message is an absolute must.

Winning enterprises realize they need special expertise to help them craft successful testimony. How can you tell if you need added assistance? If you find yourself facing one of these Seven Deadly Signs, you'd better reach for the phone right now:

1. The Oversight and Investigations Subcommittee says it has "a few small matters" it would like you to address.
2. Your CEO's lone experience as a witness was in traffic court.
3. Your government affairs team keeps using the word "punt" when advising on testimony strategy.
4. The witness for the opposition is so smooth his nickname is "Silk."
5. You have never once viewed a Congressional or legislative hearing.
6. The opposition hires numerous ex-members of Congress as "technical advisors."
7. Your research department assures you it will be "no problem" to churn out 100 pages of dense, technical testimony (better suited for use as a paperweight).

Your C-suite Is Playing a High-stakes Game

If your business is typical, you and your C-suite influencers need occasional help preparing to testify before lawmakers. In fact, you owe it to yourself and your company to seek it out if you want to emerge a winner. But where to turn? First, find an advisor who can offer a healthy dose of experience and expertise; someone who has been through the fire of tough legislative and regulatory battles.

Second, you need an expert on your side who has the knowledge to assemble and shape the facts so that your viewpoint flashes in big, bold letters. This is crucial, for witnesses who develop and use an effective message stand a far better chance of winning the grand prize. Be sure your consultant has the knowledge to help you craft a sharply-honed opening statement that sets forth a road map for the hearing, and to prepare you for a no-holds-barred question and answer session.

Third, how you look, how you speak, how you sit – even how you organize your words on the printed page – are critical factors for success. Find someone who understands these realities and who can turn them to your advantage.

Fourth, find an expert who will give you the guidance you need to improve your testimony skills. I have seen, and have helped prepare, some very good witnesses who carried the day before Congressional committees. Sad to say, I have seen many other witnesses who fell victim to one or more of the Seven Deadly Signs, embarrassing themselves and their business.

Fifth, seek out an expert who believes in preparation with regard to these basic questions:

- **Who** will testify on your behalf? Perhaps your President or CEO is the best choice, perhaps not. Whatever your decision, be sure you give it due consideration. Also, who is your audience? Gain a firm understanding of which members of Congress and which other players are important and why.

- **What** is your message? Work to assemble and deliver a clear, concise, and magnetic message.

- **When** will your campaign begin? Sure, the hearing date is set by the committee, but you must decide when to launch other outreach efforts to the media, your community, and shareholders or members.

- **Where** will you make your stand? Should you limit your efforts to the hearing itself or should you, for example, coordinate a news conference prior to the hearing?

- **Why** are you testifying? If you cannot come up with a compelling answer to this question, it might be best to decline the invitation, if possible, especially when you expect a no-win, adversarial atmosphere or you lack time to prepare. In those instances, furnish a written statement for the record.

An added thought about researching your elected officials from the American Bar Association publication "All Politics Is Local: A Practical Guide to Effective Advocacy for State and Local Bars." Dig into their motivations. Do they have an inherent interest in your issue? Specifically, how does it impact their district (never ignore pork barrel politics)? Do they have some sort of connection to your industry? Are they in the midst of a tough re-election battle? Do they have an eye on higher office? How do they get along with their legislative leadership?

Making Government Relations and Communications Play Nice Together

To face your public with a solid reputation, your entire staff needs to pull together in the same direction. As noble and straightforward as that sounds, it is a challenge for many C-suite inhabitants. Let's look at one example: You are trying to effect public policy change – perhaps advocating for new regulations or trying to prevent ill-advised legislation. Your government relations and communications teams must coordinate their activities and broadcast your message effectively to your intended audiences.

We encountered this very situation when I worked in the association world. Our officers were regularly summoned to testify on Capitol Hill. They needed formal, written testimony; a punchy oral statement; and preparation for sometimes hostile Q&A.

The standard practice had been to have the issue experts do all the work. But we weren't as effective as we might have been. Why not? Our messaging was overly complex and wonky. That's what happens when you ask technicians to develop your messages and prepare your executives to face the public. Let me be clear: Our issue staffers were some of the foremost experts in their field. Ask them a technical question and they were capable of going into great depth. But that doesn't get the job done when you have a mere five minutes to testify before Congress and an even more limited time frame to answer questions from insistent lawmakers.

How did we solve this dilemma? We put our people in positions where they were the most likely to succeed, playing to everyone's strengths. The issue experts wrote the formal, written testimony. Then we had our communications pros draft the five-minute oral statement, ensuring it was replete with our powerful messaging (which the communicators also largely developed) and written for the ear. We also ascertained that the statement was indeed five minutes long. Previously, we had run long, risking dirty looks from the members of Congress as our witnesses overshot their allotted time.

Additionally, our government relations and communications teams collaborated on the testimony preparation workshop. We jointly drew up questions our officers might hear from the legislators, and provided message-oriented responses.

Admittedly, this was not an easy sell. Some staff members took umbrage at an encroachment upon what heretofore had been their turf. And no doubt there are organizations where the communications department would shun this responsibility, claiming they already have too much on their plates.

The best response to all this is to keep the spotlight on your witnesses. A message-driven approach makes their job more straightforward. As a result, your business and public policy goals become more attainable. Shouldn't that be the bottom line?

Your strategic communications and advocacy efforts can take many forms. For instance, you can forge coalitions with like-minded businesses, interest groups, and non-profit organizations.

It also serves you well to build bridges to your peers in disciplines beyond government relations. Fellow executives who concentrate on compliance, finance, human resources, marketing, operations, procurement, risk, and technology can not only support you when the need arises, they can also serve as an early warning system on issues bubbling under the surface. Your aim is to cultivate relationships that are respectful, seamless, and mutually beneficial.

Who's for You? Who's Against You?

You also need to identify and categorize those policymakers who support you, oppose you, and remain undecided. The most straightforward means of doing this is the old campaign method of ranking supporters from 1 to 5. Here's how it works:

- **True fans**. These are your diehard advocates. They agree with your stance nearly 100 percent of the time, and will forcefully and publicly support you. They are loyal to your product, will write letters on your behalf, and follow your lead. Don't take these folks for granted. Do everything you can to help them help you, but don't spend an inordinate amount of time with them either. You've already persuaded them.

- **Friends**. This cohort tends to like you, and favors your goals. They are not, however, likely to go out of their way to vocally trumpet their support, nor are they overly passionate about you. Provide them with lots of care and feeding. You don't want to lose them.

- **Fence sitters**. These are the undecideds. Maybe they like you, maybe they don't. They can be swayed in one direction or another. They may know very little about your issues, and may not care all that much. Your job is to tip them over to your side. The 2s and 3s are where you should spend most of your time and energies.

- **Skeptics**. This group is normally against you. They are not especially hostile, but they rarely match up with your goals. They are likely to oppose you, though are not a lost cause. There may be some ways you can work together, and they may be open to compromise on certain aspects of the issue. Don't ignore them, but don't spin your wheels here either.

- **Adversaries**. Forget about this segment. They will never support you and will work actively to undermine your efforts. This group is a lost cause. Monitor their activities in the interest of opposition research, but don't waste time or resources trying to persuade them.

Another path to policymakers is the one-sheet leave behind. This little document stands to pack a lot of punch. You can leave a printed copy when you visit policymakers, send it as an email attachment to their staffers and to your advocates, place it on your website, distribute it on digital media, and record it to video and audio.

Media briefings surrounding your public policy efforts can take many forms. Hold a news conference. Initiate a series of one-on-one deskside chats with key reporters. Reach out to the trade press that covers your issues with a series of slices of your issue. Contact influential and reputable bloggers. Undertake a radio talk show or podcast campaign (see Chapter Three for greater depth on media relations).

As you consider a public policy push, you have some decisions to make. Is it best to fly solo or to build an alliance? Do you stand to gain more from negotiating or an in-your-face approach? What gets you the most bang for your buck – relying on your grassroots activists, noted experts, back room prowess, a media campaign, advertising, or any number of other techniques? Also decide who your best messengers are, and note that they may be different emissaries for different audiences.

Liaison with academics and with industry notables who have written and spoken positively about your subject. Think tanks can also be a part of this process. Organize forums and invite them to speak to share their expertise and lend legitimacy to your viewpoint. Celebrities and local influencers can play roles here, too.

Collaborating with an association to which your company belongs can also increase your strength. Just be sure that, if the issue affects your company specifically, you create your own set of background materials. Your association can back you up with issue briefs, other support vehicles, and resources (such as access to top consultants). You still need to do the heavy lifting.

Five for the Future

Your advocacy efforts can now move on to a higher plane if you use the prescriptions in Chapter Five. The key now is to move forward on those strategies. Use these "Five for the Future" discussion questions to help you sustain your C-suite's influence over the long run. Discuss these issues with co-workers, professional colleagues, mentors, and in your own mind:

1. What types of public policy advocacy campaigns should you undertake?
2. If Congress or a state legislature called your business to testify today, are you ready? Or do you need to schedule a testimony training workshop now as a first step?
3. How tough are your adversaries (these are the 5s outlined earlier in this chapter)?
4. What are three specific points you can use from Mark Zuckerberg's testimony to aid your company's efforts?
5. If you had five minutes with your member of Congress, what would you say?

Bonus content

Congressional testimony. It's the most important business meeting you'll ever have. How can you increase your company's odds for success? Gain some extra pointers at www.barkscomm.com/APlusBonus for your free copy of "Winning at the Witness Table: 60 Tips to Terrific Testimony."

CHAPTER 6

THE LONG RUN

What percentage of media training participants call for more learning upon the completion of a workshop? I've asked that question of colleagues. It often elicits a thoughtful pause. Maybe that is due to the fact that they were trying to calculate percentages, or they may never have considered the question before (which would be another indicator of the low priority given to a comprehensive and sustained professional development program).

The disparity in numbers of media training participants who request added learning afterward is broad. Interestingly, those who answer this question quickly and firmly typically reply, "zero" – in other words, no one ever seeks out ongoing improvement. On the other end of the scale, I've found the high range sits at 80 percent asking for some type of follow-up learning. Other respondents run the gamut in between, with a concentration at the low end of the range.

A workshop that does little more than cycle through a litany of generic mock interviews may, in the end, actually hamper lifelong learning.

A well-planned, strategic methodology, on the other hand, could result in new, more effective messaging techniques or information about specific journalists or publications in order to pursue more media coverage.

How can you communicate what type of return on investment (ROI) media training delivers? Of more importance, how do extended training opportunities provide ROI? When the term "return on investment" is uttered, many executives think only of dollar signs. Yet there are other equally important measurements – reputation, positioning vis-à-vis competitors in the marketplace, and career advancement – to name just a few.

I am chagrined to report that it is rare to hear from a participant after the session. This begs a series of questions: Is this due to the fact that the consultants don't even try? Is it something inherent in current approaches to training? Are there institutional roadblocks that need to be torn down?

More Questions than Answers

What accounts for the disparity in the percentages of those asking for sustained professional development? Does it have anything to do with the type of individual involved? For example, is there a difference in outlook between those who work for large corporations versus smaller businesses or non-profit organizations? Is it something specific to the organizational differences among such entities? Might the perspective of scientists differ from that of marketers who, in turn, differ from accountants or various other professions?

Is it the consultant's approach? What is the correlation between the consultant's point of view and how many participants ask for added learning? Is it because the consultant neglects to emphasize it? Or does the consultant fail to emphasize it because his client base has demonstrated over time an indifference to lifelong learning and he has given up in frustration?

Here's Why Your Business Might Fail

Answers to these questions might involve several factors:

Inexperience: Some communications practitioners simply don't have enough time in the trenches to understand the value of a sustained program. **Solution**: These folks need a separate professional development plan for themselves. Until they can get up to speed (and yes, this takes years), bring on board a wise hand who can speak truth to your C-suite while mentoring less experienced colleagues.

Incompetence: Let's face reality. Some people just aren't that smart. And some have natural talents in areas other than communications and public affairs. **Solution**: Examine your staffing patterns and hiring practices. You may need to make some changes. But ask yourself this: Would you prefer to put your business and career at risk?

Indifference: These folks are checked out. Maybe they're just waiting for their retirement date to arrive or they are new to your company and have discovered they really don't like their job. **Solution**: Again, pay attention to who you bring on board. This group can cause more damage than any other since they may actively work to sabotage your communications strategy.

Ignorance: A cousin of incompetence above, these individuals go through the motions blissfully unaware of how to address communications concerns. **Solution**: They may just need some guidance. They are likely intelligent enough to understand. Perhaps no one has taken the time to show them the ropes or explain the bigger picture.

Budget: Among those businesses that hesitate to implement a cohesive program, I have found over the years that a perceived lack of funds is the most common excuse. Sometimes it's probably even true. **Solution**: Reframe the question and ask yourself, how much is my company's reputation – in some cases its very existence – worth? And when it comes to the careers of your C-suite inhabitants (as well as your very own job), isn't it worth spending a bit more coin now to avoid trouble down the road? As an old TV commercial about the need for changing your car's oil used to say, "You can pay me now or you can pay me later." Fact: Later costs a lot more, both in terms of budget and reputation.

What does all of this mean? A company-wide, sustained professional development program is essential if your business plans to rise to the top and stay there. It also means that you need buy-in at every level. Everyone from the CEO to your most junior worker deserves a plan capable of sharpening their communications edge.

C-suite Executives as Learners

I really enjoy speaking in public. You have probably guessed that already.

Despite delivering many a presentation through the years, I am constantly struck by how many people come up to chat afterward and tell me, in so many words, how smart I am. No braggadocio intended. It's a function of viewing the person in the front of the room as the font of all wisdom.

How to deal with such flattery? Of course, "Thank you" is always a good start. Another idea: I mention that I often learn as much as teach. It's important to keep in mind that communications is a two-way street, even when speaking before a large group there to gain your expertise.

To cite one example, one audience I addressed eagerly participated in an exercise designed to arrive at solutions that can help persuade reluctant leaders to sharpen their communications edge (the talk was titled "What to Do When the Boss Says No." Thanks to this talented group of professionals, I gained some new ideas to incorporate into future strategic consulting opportunities. Some of the accumulated gems:

- Gain reinforcement from the boss' peers, both internal and external.

- Encourage them to engage in self-assessment, and offer tools to do so.
- Seek access through their administrative assistants when you find the door shut (literally or figuratively).
- Insist on an ongoing program that improves their communications skills.

The larger lesson for all of us: Attune yourself to the moments during your presentations that can enhance your lifelong learning, then use them to build upon the knowledge you can deliver to others.

Okay, So Burn Me at the Stake

Sustained professional development programs are best for achieving long-term effects. Such an approach helps to achieve long run benefits like a shinier reputation, a promotion on the job, victory before lawmakers and regulators.

Too often the focus is on a one-time affair. Many involved with communications strategy and training view me as a heretic due to my insistence that a single consultation, in and of itself, is of relatively little long-term value. It is more tactical than strategic.

Here's even more sacrilege: Much media training as practiced today is largely ineffective. Why? Many workshops fail to provide a plan for continued long-term business and career success. Furthermore, they neglect to address ROI, both for the executives individually and for their businesses.

What action can consultants, internal communicators, and participants take to achieve more positive and long-lasting results? All parties are encouraged to maximize the return on their investment by making use of the best practice recommendations. These steps can include anything from a round of formal refresher workshops to creative telephone consultations to suggesting exercises individuals can do independently.

Even among organizations that tip their caps to long-range professional and organizational goals, implementing any plan remains difficult: Participants are often left with little if any guidance. Their ongoing learning suffers, falling victim to a lack of direction and to other factors such as day-to-day professional and business demands, and diminishing motivation over time. Sure, the energy level is high at the conclusion of a workshop. But the yen to follow through fades quickly.

In today's typical media training environment, participants are often subjected to a single "one-off" session in which they are expected to learn everything in that instant. Legitimate attempts at learning how better to work with reporters are too often the exception, not the rule.

Where Do You Fit?

Over time, I've observed four philosophical categories into which C-suite officers and communicators fall:

1. **The Mover and Shaker**: Expresses frustration with the lack of leveraging communications and government relations for long-term business success, and takes action to improve the situation.

2. **The Quitter**: Realizes it is difficult to inculcate lifelong learning, and throws his hands up believing there is nothing anyone can do to make it happen.

3. **The Carefree Soul**: Recognizes it is difficult to instill lifelong learning, and is not bothered by it. In fact, she prefers one-off relationships with no follow up.

4. **The Know Nothing**: Consists of low-skill "trainers" in the marketplace, often generalists moonlighting as training consultants. These individuals may not even realize the situation exists.

Let us look into the attitudes and methods of the three main groups with a stake in a strategic approach to communications training:

1. Communications and government relations executives who counsel the C-suite.
2. Those in the C-suite who deserve comprehensive, sustained professional development.
3. Consultants who provide strategic training services.

Why Examine the Lasting Effects?

Organizations capable of delivering magnetic messages via spokespeople who exhibit sharp communications skills tend to win the day in everything from new product launches to public policy battles. Those who demonstrate solid communications skills have higher odds of achieving their professional development and career goals more quickly and effectively.

This chapter is intended to help businesses maintain momentum from their professional development endeavors by shedding light on the need for lifelong learning, and to make it more effective and efficient in two ways:

1. Unmask the current situation, making organizations and their leaders more aware of a current shortfall in many an approach to this type of learning.
2. Offer practical improvement strategies that consultants and internal communicators can put into practice immediately.

The advice outlined here proves valuable with regard to the range of communications training, including media training, public speaking workshops, and legislative testimony preparation. In fact, it also applies in such situations as staff meetings, sales pitches, fielding questions in a variety of settings, and much more.

It is interesting to note how often conversations with colleagues on this subject stray from the lasting effects and into discussions of standard tactics. Ideas surrounding development of long-term business and professional success rarely surface without prompting. It takes a concerted effort in most cases to tug the conversation back to the topic at hand. Still, I take this tendency to drift off topic as an indicator of how little lifelong learning is associated with communications training and how challenging it is to focus communicators on the need for continual improvement.

Professional Development or Check the Box?

Many C-suite inhabitants take such learning for granted. The view of media training as a "check the box" task, not a learning opportunity, does little good for two reasons:

1. There is a higher chance this check-the-box attitude will result in an inferior "off the shelf" workshop, one that is not customized to the particular individuals' needs.
2. It ignores the need to truly improve media relations abilities, instead becoming little more than an item on some bureaucratic to-do checklist.

One of the challenges is that people get wrapped up in things. They don't consciously ignore the training they have undertaken, they simply forget to implement it, given day-to-day pressures. That is why a training continuum – arranging future sessions – is important over the course of time.

Some consultants and executives view communications training as similar to a one-time seminar on a specific and narrow skill such as how to use a new app. Absorbing communications skills and messaging is different. In that seminar, once you learn the ins and outs of the app, you've got it. Internalizing best communications practices, on the other hand, is more nuanced and requires diligent and thoughtful practice.

Should We Call It Lifelong Learning?

Why do companies sign up their spokespeople for more skill building? They have more people to train, need a repeat session for those executives who require more attention, or seek to refine already solid skills. Individuals who come back for more add depth to how they express their message, and gain

more command, comfort, and leverage with what their message can do for them.

Some consultants fail to view lifelong learning as a topic of conversation with participants; neither the consultant nor the participant thinks of media training in that way. Indeed, there are sometimes visceral negative reactions to the mere use of the term "lifelong learning." Perhaps the definition of Eurofound (the European Foundation for the Improvement of Living and Working Conditions, a European Union body), provides a better approach. It describes lifelong learning as "all learning activity undertaken throughout life, with the aim of improving knowledge, skills and competence within a personal, civic, social and/or employment-related perspective."

Your business must decide which is the right avenue for you. When seeking outside assistance, it would be wise to ask prospective consultants about their long-term approach, and its return on investment as it relates to your company's goals and the individual participant's career objectives. Examine the four categories listed above, (the Mover and Shaker, the Quitter, the Carefree Soul, the Know Nothing), decide which philosophy best suits your needs, and seek out a consultant whose belief system mirrors yours.

The Consultant's Responsibility

Training consultants can – and bear a responsibility to – motivate extended learning by suggesting specific steps, both formal and informal. Participants need insights into why they need to practice after their workshop, understanding that it is not simply training for its own sake. This follow-up must be customized for each individual. It boils down to learning from your own performance, both in real-life interviews and in the workshop, and understanding the areas where improvement is necessary.

This individualized approach must be based on real-world considerations. These are, after all, business executives concerned with the bottom line. Their programs must offer everyday benefits, not espouse an airy, philosophical tone.

Though it will certainly take time and effort to shift this perspective, one relatively easy fix is for your consultant to emphasize the concrete benefits of ongoing learning – from a brighter career path to better news clips – with everyone in the company, from initial contacts in the communications or public affairs shop to the C-suite dwellers, vice presidents, directors, and managers who partake of the learning.

Part of this can be done verbally. For instance, conversations with consultants should assume that follow-up learning is a normal part of the mix. Some of the attitude adjustment can be done in written form. Preparatory materials for participants, for example, should include reference to how they are expected to extend their learning over time.

Leaders embrace next steps when they see practical applications in their daily lives. Consider, for instance, the connection one executive made between skills he learned to be interviewed on the Today Show and his later efforts at pitching an editor with an article idea. Another example is the corporate CEO who applied the communication principles learned in his training for a CNBC interview to help him run more efficient staff meetings.

Consultants owe it to their clients to devote conscious forethought and planning when it comes to advancing their students' learning over time. They also, I would argue, bear an ethical responsibility to do so.

Plan for Success

This fact raises one area for improvement that is fairly straightforward: Consultants should build in to the planning process for every engagement a means for extending your C-suite's learning beyond the day of the workshop. Further, they should reinforce its importance throughout the session with such techniques as offering an opportunity to revisit matters in person or over the telephone following their next media interview.

Semantics matter (as all communications strategy consultants should know well). Executives might be resistant to training once they have participated in one workshop. Instead of suggested additional "training," words like "refresher" or "update" can keep things on a positive note, prevent them from thinking they may have done something wrong, and offer an ego boost.

When the day of the workshop arrives, it is recommended that consultants raise two issues with participants at the beginning of the session (naturally, advance consultation with the client is strongly advised to ensure there is support for these moves):

Schedule a later session at a date certain to reinforce learning. The date may range from one week to one year, depending on the participants' needs.

Emphasize the ROI that flows from the training workshop.

Beating Executives over the Head

Understanding that there is more to ROI than mere dollars, one technique involves showing a video clip with a poor interview subject, telling participants, "Don't let this be you." Seeing fellow C-level leaders flub an interview demonstrates in concrete terms that it can happen to them, too.

All of which raises another important point. Too many workshops focus solely on correcting problem areas. Or, as I often say more colloquially, too many consultants walk into the room intent only on hitting the executive over the head with a two-by-four when they make mistakes. This emphasis on weaknesses is a rocky path to learning for most of us.

While minimizing missteps in the press clearly matters, learning is more readily accomplished by concentrating on strengths. What does the participant do well and how can that be drawn out during interviews with reporters? The lesson here is to also show them interviews that lead to positive outcomes.

It is true that some C-suiters aren't terribly self-introspective. They think like actor Al Pacino: "My weaknesses ... I wish I could come up with something. I'd probably have the same pause if you asked me what my strengths are. Maybe they're the same thing." Your consultant must be skilled at extracting those qualities from your executives, then getting them to act.

Another hurdle for consultants is to blend a focus on utilizing strengths with a longer range plan to correct challenges. This applies particularly to dealings with strong-willed senior executives who expect rigorous critiques on what they need to improve as opposed to what they do well. Thus, the consultant bears responsibility not only for sharpening participants' communications skills in the long run, but, at the same time, encouraging them to learn more efficiently.

Many senior executives already have a solid grasp on the basics of media relations. Rather than a learning experience that scans the horizon, these more advanced learners need to deal with specific, individual challenges such as the need to improve brevity or eliminate jargon.

Some consultants err in making training a one-off experience when working with a highly accomplished spokesperson. Yet the fact is that they probably got really good by dedicating themselves to learning over many years. The "good ones" are the very individuals likely to crave more advice because they realize there is always room for improvement. Thus, I suggest caution if a consultant does not come forth with a plan to continue to advance even the savviest C-suite leader's performance.

Another large part of the picture: Consultants must find ways to rise to the challenge of continuing to advance their own expertise. Their professional development may be accomplished through reading, conferences, informal conversations with colleagues, research projects that stretch their horizons, membership in professional societies that feature relevant learning opportunities, or other means. This is "walking the walk." Those who advocate ongoing learning must themselves practice it in their own professional lives.

The Participant's Responsibility

No one, no matter how skilled or dedicated to lifelong learning, can force your C-suite to learn if they resist. This applies both to lessons in the workshop itself and to ongoing instruction. An executive's self-motivation and openness to learning new things plays a large role. It is only natural for spokespeople to zero in on their communications skills when a media interview is right around the corner. Similar to cramming for that college final, practice is necessary, but most people aren't going to do it without some external motivation. Also, much depends on the participant's motivation and level of regular engagement with the media. Consultants would be wise to ask in advance of a workshop what participants expect to do with the training, why they were nominated for the training session, and why they care (are they up for a promotion? Will they get fired if they fail to take part?).

The Company's Responsibility

One key to comprehensive, sustained professional development is the active involvement of senior internal public affairs/communications and, where applicable, investor relations staff. It is these individuals who will have day-to-day contact with your executives after the workshop. Their role in creating a culture of lifelong learning cannot be emphasized enough. These internal experts need to build a culture that is receptive to ongoing professional development. Using an analogy from the health care field, it demands a chronic outlook.

Formal systems to ensure the organization's spokespeople get better over time are often lacking. Oh, there might be the occasional query of the communications shop as certain cases arise, but improvement comes in a scattershot way, through real-world experience. While that experience is helpful, relying on learning under pressure may not be ideal.

Left unsaid is the idea that the weakest spokespeople are the least likely to appreciate and utilize learning opportunities. The organization faces a choice with those individuals: Either put them on an accelerated, sustained learning track capable of improving their performance or minimize their interactions with the media and the public.

Choosing the Right Consultant

When turning to consultants with special expertise in media training, organizations have a vast array of choices available to them, simply because every consultant has a different philosophical approach to the workshop as a whole and to its effectiveness relative to lifelong learning.

This makes it incumbent upon the organization to perform adequate due diligence when selecting its preferred consultant. Part of that due diligence means asking questions:

- What types of lifelong learning resources (if any) does he offer?
- Has he authored books and training guides or does he instead rely on a sheaf of copies stapled together?
- Does the proposal or contract contain language that solidifies his commitment to improving participants' skills over time or is it silent on that matter?
- Does he emphasize follow-up workshops, telephone consultations, or e-learning?
- What training modules has he developed that are designed to further learning over the long run?

While your preferred answers to these questions may differ from that of other businesses, it is advisable to clarify ahead of time what is important to you. This helps to ensure that you get the type of program you want and to avoid misunderstandings.

The Public Company Effect

Communicators who work for public companies and, in particular, those that operate in regulated environments face extra challenges. In an often changing regulatory landscape, the communicator must carve out time to make sure the messages are in place.

All members of the corporate C-suite should participate in comprehensive communications training to prepare for potential crises before they occur. Such inoculation provides a reasoned method of learning over time. Heavily regulated industries like health care, pharmaceuticals, biotechnology, and financial services would be wise to place added emphasis on their spokespeople's lifelong learning so as to keep pace with constant change, ensure up-to-date messaging, and stay out of regulatory hot water.

How Much Is Too Much?

One obvious means of extending learning beyond a single workshop is to add on a second workshop at a later date. For example, the first may concentrate on basic skills while future sessions might take place every time an earnings report comes up or to hash out messaging for emerging issues. As an alternative, it is possible to hold hour-long sessions for larger groups at larger corporate or association meetings. The format can consist of an introduction to dealing with the media or a more advanced approach that gives participants the third degree.

Some businesses schedule workshops on at least an annual basis. From a business and client relationship perspective, however, added workshops are not always practical or viewed kindly. Indeed, recommending no more than additional formal workshops – admittedly a high-ticket service – can be viewed by clients as little more than a means for the consultant to pad his bill.

Assembling an effective and sustained learning program can be a tightrope walk for consultants. Those who recommend ongoing learning are not in all cases merely seeking an added revenue stream, though that may sometimes be the case. You are the best judge of that.

The issue of resources also comes into play, particularly in times when some companies have slashed training budgets. One-trick pony consultants who offer only one service – a formal workshop – are not putting their clients first and face the risk of running their own businesses into the ground.

When discussing lifelong learning techniques, rarely do I turn to online tools such as webcasts or self-study programs. Online learning is not useful when it comes to media relations, public speaking, or advocacy efforts due to a lack of real-time interaction and the need for "laying on of hands," as I like to call it.

The Bottom Line

Media training must deliver return on investment – an investment that bolsters long-term success for the company and career success for the executive. Yet in its current state, it too often fails that test due to a lack of emphasis on learning over the long run.

C-suiters who endorse training for their firms have the right to expect a more effective approach. The ROI they seek is not limited to dollars. It may be measured in anything from reputation to risk avoidance to the ability of an up-and-coming executive to expand her skill set in preparation for a step up the corporate ladder.

Even businesses that acknowledge the need to strive for such long-range professional and organizational goals find it difficult to implement learning over time, as participants are often provided little long-term guidance. As business magnate Estée Lauder said of her success, "I didn't get there by wishing for it or hoping for it, but by working for it."

The current environment is replete with single, "one-off" training engagements. While this type of limited learning can be of some use to spokespeople, the evolution of their skills suffers for lack of sustained attention.

Fortunately, following the concrete steps outlined below can bestow more positive and long-lasting business and career success upon consultants, internal communicators, and the C-suite.

Best Practice Recommendations

Use this catalog of follow-up learning methods designed to help your company achieve the long-term business and career goals you want to attain from your communications professional development program. It is highly recommended that consultants and internal communicators implement the approaches that make sense for each C-suite individual:

- Close every workshop with personalized, customized next steps.
- Emphasize that this is not a "here today, gone tomorrow" approach during the initial session.
- Schedule multiple learning opportunities at the very beginning of the planning process.
- Make it clear that meetings should be scheduled throughout the coming year, even if only for 15 minutes on the telephone.
- Convene a workshop devoted strictly to messaging.
- Hold regularly scheduled refreshers.
- Set up as needed "just in time" sessions to deal with issues that arise.
- Conduct follow-up sessions to deal with a crisis.
- Give them easy to use and specific role play exercises they can practice with colleagues when time permits.
- Offer quick-hitting instructional sessions via telephone.
- Underscore the value of applying techniques learned in a media training workshop in other areas of professional life, such as delivering presentations, dealing with policymakers, and running meetings.
- Provide ongoing email counsel.
- Offer examples of spokespeople who started poorly but improved over time.
- Review periodically the video of exercises conducted during their workshop.
- Emphasize that the training represents a long-term investment in the future of their career and their company's reputation.

- Conduct occasional role plays in their work environment.
- Present them with a toolkit to take home.
- Give them exercises they can do in a flash to sharpen skills.
- Provide a workbook so even if they have only 15 minutes to practice in a given week, they can make an appointment with themselves.
- Conduct periodic mock telephone interviews with an ex-reporter who writes an article based on the conversation.
- Write a report that includes assessment of the existing situation, growth noted during the session, and common sense improvement strategies to pursue.
- Work through a specific question the participant has difficulty dealing with.
- Offer a one-hour session for larger groups that serves as an introductory learning vehicle.
- Hold group sessions that put participants on the hot seat.
- Leave them with examples of successful interviews.
- Offer additional workshops that focus on specific bloggers and other digital media writers.
- Provide a notebook in which they can write about media interviews they observe with a mind toward the quotable quotes. What is that one sound bite that makes the cut, and why? Many spokespeople struggle with this.
- Organize a session on the changing journalism landscape.
- Laminate a small tip sheet to carry in their wallet.
- Give them pre-assignments they are expected to complete in advance of their next workshop.

In the interest of furthering this research, I urge you to contact me with additional methods that can be added to future editions.

Enduring Professional Development

Communications executive: "My CEO has already been 'media trained."

Me: "Glad to hear it. When was that?"

Executive: "Oh, four or five years ago when she first came on board."

Me: "And you've encountered no new issues since then?"

Executive: "Well ... "

Me: "How has your CEO grown in the job?"

Executive: "She has a much better grasp of our company, our people, and our industry."

Me: "Tell me how her ability to deliver your company's messages has grown."

Executive: "Um ... "

To protect clients, this is a composite rather than a verbatim conversation. The point is it is an all too common belief that, once an individual has experienced one communications training workshop, he has accumulated all the knowledge necessary for the remainder of his career.

When you fail to aid in sharpening your C-suite's communications edge, you're dodging a critical professional duty. As former Texas Gov. Ann Richards said, "If you think taking care of yourself is selfish, change your mind. If you don't, you're simply ducking your responsibilities."

Think of it this way. Would you entrust your health to a doctor who graduated medical school and called it a day in terms of his continuing medical education? How about having that veteran accountant do your taxes with the benefit of no added learning since earning an undergraduate degree a few decades ago? I suspect we'd soon see you in the emergency room with an undetected condition or behind bars for tax evasion.

So it goes with communicating your company's messages to your public through the media, in presentations, and before elected officials. A single communications training workshop is inadequate if you don't implement a follow-up plan for learning over time.

How do you make that happen? Try these ideas:

- Plan your training program to ensure your communications efforts support your C-suite's long-term professional and organizational goals. Yes, you must build your business goals into the planning process for every session, and make sure your internal communications team and your consultant follow through.
- To raise the odds for reaching those important goals, extend your professional development efforts beyond one single day. Set up a system that offers your C-suite more skill-building opportunities, both from your consultant and your internal communications staff.
- Make it clear to your spokespeople that ongoing skill sharpening leads to better career options for them.
- Refuse to work with consultants who think learning involves only browbeating your executives. Secure a long-term relationship with a pro who knows how to elicit strengths and help address challenges over the long run.

- Video is one of the best lifelong learning tools, so record all exercises during your practice sessions. And don't ignore video afterward. Suggest that your C-suite learners review it occasionally to aid in the ongoing quest for improvement.
- Lastly (ignore this one at your own peril), enlist your CEO in improving your strategic communications efforts. Emphasize to her the need for your program to support your long-term business success and the career paths of your spokespeople. Your efforts may be doomed without this support from the top.

Chart Your Course for Lifelong Learning

He's Mr. Know-it-all. He may be your boss, a colleague in another department, or the guy you work with on a community project. He's the guy Harry Truman had in mind when he said, "The only things worth learning are the things you learn after you know it all."

He truly believes that his learning curve stopped when he earned his degree. That was a fine attitude in the long ago and far away. In today's competitive environment, however, it is a recipe for professional and personal failure.

Everyone from lawyers to auto mechanics realizes that lifelong learning is vital to success. Shrewd C-suite influencers also understand the need to sharpen their communications edge at every opportunity.

There are some real costs for business leaders who receive an "F" on their communications report card. Their enterprises suffer lower revenues, lost sales, and a poor public image. For non-profit organizations, it means lower membership numbers and fewer donations. Personally, poor communicators miss out on the best jobs and plum promotions.

The hallmark of success in today's climate is a perpetual stream of instruction that sharpens knowledge, skills, and competence over the long run. But it will only bear fruit if you agree to embrace learning with a positive attitude and a thirst for knowledge. Deny that, and you will soon witness your peers zipping past you on the career ladder.

This applies to the business as well. The enterprise with the most current knowledge generally wins. If you fail to engage – and engage your C-suite – in a culture of lifelong learning, it won't be long until you are tagged a failure.

How do you develop this thirst? First of all, make learning pleasurable. This is a matter of winning a new job or leadership position within your community, not being assigned a dry term paper by a cranky high school English teacher.

Sustained professional development comes easiest when you focus on what you are good at and what you enjoy. Research shows that is where your improvement comes most readily.

Achieve your goals by establishing a lifelong learning plan. Here are some questions to help guide you:

- Which current strengths do I want to sharpen?
- How do I find the cream of the crop and screen out the plethora of bogus information?
- What are my speaking goals – giving a report to a half-dozen co-workers every Monday morning or addressing large halls with thousands of people?
- What formats feel most natural – small group presentations using an outline? Slide shows? Participation on a panel?
- Over time, which areas of weakness do I want to work to improve?
- How can my professional development plan broaden my reach as a communicator, such as making pitches to my board, dealing with the media, or testifying before legislative and regulatory bodies?

Take no heed of Mr. Know-it-all. Focus on your own dreams. A solid and sustained professional development plan paves the way.

When Time for Learning Is Tight

Nothing compares to simulations and their face-to-face approach to learning. While experience has made me a firm believer that this laying on of hands represents the best option, there are certain situations in which remote solutions can advance your cause.

A telephone session is a nice fit when time is tight. If you have scheduled a high-stakes media interview in the next 24 hours, you may not have sufficient time for a complete media training workshop. In that instance, a telephone review presents a flexible alternative.

Here's another example: Your CFO has plenty of experience and media savvy, but she needs a refresher course for an interview crucial to the success of an upcoming media campaign. Again, a highly individualized telephone or Skype consultation offers an effective solution. Such a session answers the bell when you have an interview with a key reporter at hand. It helps you square your messages so that they resonate with the journalist. Plus, it allows time for a practice interview or two.

There are other situations in which this type of remote learning proves valuable. For instance, you may want to test how your story will play out in the press. Many businesses think that their messages are solid and that their

C-suite has committed to delivering them at every turn. But will a reporter think so? Some telephone-based exercises provide the true test.

Your consultant should be able to bring on board a former reporter to conduct a telephone interview with your C-suite, just like a real reporter would (then again, if you're working with a solid media strategy consultant, he has experience as a reporter). As an ex-journalist, he knows the techniques and tricks reporters use when they fire questions at their subjects. The reporter writes a news article based on the interview, then emails it to the interviewee. The real value comes in the performance debrief. Make sure you find someone capable of offering a no-holds-barred assessment that contains valuable strategies for immediate improvement.

This approach works for the experienced news source seeking to sharpen her skills to prepare for an important interview. It also demonstrates to those C-suiters who are less accustomed to dealing with reporters how they can successfully navigate the sometimes rocky journalistic shoals.

I remain convinced that the in-person approach makes for the most effective learning environment. But if you need a rapid response solution, a telephone session can help fulfill your needs in certain specific cases.

Create Your Own Professional Development Plan

Ongoing professional improvement involves a constant commitment to your personal education. One core value I try to instill in every client early in our relationship is a commitment to develop a plan that serves them well in weeks, months, and years to come.

How can you achieve your own system that best suits your business? Foster this desire for ongoing learning through your personal experiences as well as through reading, observing, and listening. Keep your mind open to those learning moments that spring up at the most unexpected times and places. Perhaps you happen upon an article that strikes you as particularly insightful; share it with your C-suite. You may attend a relevant presentation or observe a worthy media interview; mention a tip or two to them. Or you might gain an idea on the spur of the moment from a colleague; pass it along to your executives. Such instances will crop up as you walk through life. Stay attuned to them.

Fostering a culture of learning is not always an easy sell. That is why it makes sense to start small to get an idea of how attuned your officers are. Review past clips, speeches, and Congressional testimony appearances with them. Chat them up in casual situations about the strength of your organizational messages. Ask them what type of media interviews they find most comfortable.

Watch others as they communicate in public situations, not with the intent to mimic, but with the curiosity that will aid your ability to counsel your C-suite by noting positives as well as gaffes.

You are in school for the rest of your life: Communications school. This educational institution is one without walls, without report cards, and without grades. You have the benefit of being able to spend your time learning whatever you want to learn whenever you want to learn it and at whatever pace you choose. Think how overjoyed we would have been to have such possibilities as high schoolers.

Dedicate time to learning what you need to walk tall down your chosen path, whether that be a better job, a shinier public image for your company, higher status as a community leader, success in winning elective office, or any other goal that is important to you. "You can't be that kid standing at the top of the water slide, overthinking it. You have to go down the chute," exhorts comedian Tina Fey.

Commit to curiosity. Read the great speeches from history. Ask questions of dedicated communications experts and read what they have to say.

One note of caution: Be sure to vet your sources carefully. There is a lot of bad advice out there, especially online, but also in books and articles. Lifelong learning involves understanding how to separate real gold from fool's gold.

Five for the Future

A sustained professional development program for your C-suite is imperative, as you discovered in Chapter Six. The trick is putting that strategy into practice. Use these "Five for the Future" discussion questions to help you sustain your C-suite's influence over the long run. Discuss these issues with co-workers, professional colleagues, mentors, and in your own mind:

1. What arguments can you use to persuade your C-suite to follow through and become stellar communicators?
2. What steps can you take to establish stronger relationships with the C-suite's executive assistants? How can you enlist them to schedule practice time on your leaders' calendars?
3. How does a continuous professional development regimen accrue to your company's bottom line? Remember to examine more than just the financial aspects; also consider your reputational and public policy bottom lines.
4. Given the hectic calendars your C-suite maintains, what types of learning opportunities can you devise that fit into their schedules?
5. How can you become an advocate within your industry for ongoing professional development?

Bonus content

Hands-on counsel works best with your C-suite. Discover how to set up an experiential learning plan by visiting www.barkscomm.com/APlusBonus for your copy of "Simulations Generate Communications Success."

CHAPTER 7

COMMUNICATIONS TRAINING

This is a story about the perils of not inculcating your executives effectively. A global public relations agency that I consult for regularly once asked me to lead a media training workshop for the CEO of a Fortune 100 company. It involved a crisis situation surrounding problems with the company's manufacturing process, leading to a product recall. The CEO was far from a stellar communicator. To make matters worse, his communications team seemed intimidated and, therefore, impotent to encourage his further professional development. Sadly, the agency cancelled the workshop at the client's behest. Two days later, the predictable occurred when the CEO held his news conference. The next day's edition of *The Wall Street Journal* contained quotes from him maligning his own products.

How can you avoid these goofs when counseling your C-suite? First, work to instill a sense of lifelong learning. Depending on your CEO's attitude, this can be a formal program or a more informal approach.

Regardless of your executives' take on the need for media training, it falls to you to connect the dots for them if you hope to stake a legitimate claim to your seat at the decision-making table. Your choices are a) counsel them honestly, b) remain content to toil for a second-rate organization (and rightly be accused of professional malpractice), or c) look for another job.

The CEO who has not bought into the need for sustained improvement may try to shoot the messenger, in this case the chief communications officer (CCO) who must honestly and accurately report bad tidings. On the other hand, CEOs committed to enhancing the skills of their workers trust that CCO whether they deliver positive or negative news. If your leader falls into the latter category, congratulations.

Peer-to-peer pressure can be highly motivating, so work to leverage your star C-level communicators in an effort to persuade their reluctant counterparts.

Once you have broken the ice, you are ready to move on to next learning steps:

- Consulting them on media, speaking, and public policy opportunities.
- Including them at the appropriate time during your message development sessions.
- Conducting Q&A drills, tossing questions at them to see how they deliver your messages.
- Holding mini-seminars focusing on areas they need to reinforce or sharpen.

Once you set some groundwork, it is time to organize a series of professional development workshops. If you have neither the skills nor the discipline to handle this internally (don't be embarrassed; most corporations don't), hire a consultant with requisite expertise.

The research tells us that connecting communications to the C-suite matters to senior communicators. You are the one charged with forging that connection in your organization.

You Have Got to Be Kidding Me

It comes as a surprise to many of my clients. They sometimes blink when they learn I spend far more time preparing their media training for their C-suite executives than leading the workshop itself.

There is a lot to pull together if a program is to prove of strategic benefit. The groundwork can be broken down into five main categories:

1. Prepare the participants.
2. Prepare your training consultant.
3. Prepare other internal staff.
4. Prepare the training facility.
5. Prepare the training agenda.

We will review each separately, revealing steps your business can take to achieve a professional development experience that is as smooth and headache-free as possible.

Prepare the Participants

There are both logistical and psychological concerns to consider when priming those who will actively participate in the workshop. It is vital to ensure communication flows in both directions to motivate them to attend and to assuage any hesitation they may harbor.

Once the participants have been identified, they should receive two documents, one informational, the other intended to solicit information from them. This underscores the two-way communication channel, getting the C-suite comfortable providing information and realizing they are empowered to ask any questions they may have. It also gives them their first glimpse into the training consultant, and his style and approach.

The informational document explains what they can expect during their workshop. This is particularly important for those who have never experienced media training before. The entire notion may seem foreign and, in some cases, a bit scary. Some in leadership may feel they are being targeted because they have done something wrong when dealing with reporters in the past.

The fact is most people are chosen to participate because they already reside in your C-suite or they have been identified as potential rising stars. And sometimes larger group programs are held to identify which individuals are best suited to dealing with the media (and which should be kept far away from the microphone and the reporter's notebook). Remedial sessions do happen, but they are – and should remain – the distinct minority. The cold, harsh reality: If you have a chronic underperformer talking to the press, it is best to cut your losses, reassign him, and groom someone else to fill that critical role.

Paint a Vivid Picture

What should your information document contain? First, outline for your experts what they can expect during their workshop, tailoring the information to your specific situation. I like to point out that this will be a customized learning experience tailored to their needs.

You can explain that it will be devoted to development of key messages, that they will be interviewed on camera by an ex-reporter (yes, your workshop leader should be a former reporter), and that all exercises will be recorded to video, played back, and critiqued. While this may seem clear to you and me, I have seen shocked looks on the faces of participants when they first caught sight of a camera upon entering the training facility.

Offer a bit of background about your consultant, perhaps providing them with his biographical sketch or a reference to his website. At the very least, advise them that they will be studying with a communications veteran who focuses on teaching today's leaders how to communicate with the public (as part of your due diligence, make sure your consultant is a subject matter expert, not a jack of all trades masquerading as an authority).

When I lead a professional development session, I like to let participants know in advance that they will begin to shape a system designed to help them work with the media more effectively over the long haul. Some consultants deemphasize this aspect. I agree with Albert Einstein, who said, "Education is what remains after one has forgotten what one has learned in school." Ongoing learning is critical to ongoing success.

Along these same lines, tell your leaders what, if any, types of take home resources you plan to give them. Books, guides, a video library of their mock interviews, and follow-up contact with their consultant fall into this category.

In your informational document, I also recommend pointing out what media training is not. For example, it is not a quick fix that provides everything they need to know in a single day. Also, it is not a place for those who lack commitment to learning how to more effectively deal with the press. Nor is it a substitute office to deal with phone calls, emails, text messages, or Twitter. And by all means, it should not be viewed as something they do just for appearance sake. If you get a sense that one or more of your participants does not want to be part of the learning experience, let them take a pass. No point in poisoning the atmosphere for those who are eager to sharpen their communications edge.

Gaining Initial Feedback

The second document – the one soliciting information – takes the form of a questionnaire that probes a number of areas regarding their experience with the media to date. It should also be designed to unearth attitudes and biases toward the press. Some training consultants look for this, others don't. My belief is failing to gain these attitudinal insights is akin to wearing blinders. But you must decide whether this is important to your business and its communication objectives when you select your consultant.

What questions are found on the feedback form? They should vary depending on your specific business goals as they relate to issues surrounding this particular session. At the same time, there are certain core questions you likely will want to ask on every occasion.

Begin with what benefits they want to gain, and ask them to be as specific as possible. This will help your workshop leader fine-tune the curriculum to a much more personalized level. Also get a sense of how much experience they have had in serving as a spokesperson before the media, what

types of media they typically interact with, and how they would characterize their performance.

Learn if they have participated in previous media training workshops. Next, ask for their general impression of reporters, then dig a bit deeper and discern whether there are any reporters they believe are biased one way or the other as it affects your company.

Don't forget to probe for "angels" and "devils" – other news sources who would support your position or try to tear down your arguments. Ask if there are any situations, real or potential, that would make them uncomfortable. Again, your consultant needs to know about such items to smoke them out in the safety and security of the training environment.

Finish with an open-ended question that asks whether there is anything else they want to share. Responses here can be revealing at times.

Prepare Your Strategic Training Consultant

There are a number of basic items your consultant will need to see as he strategizes. For instance, give him a rundown on your participants' communications strengths and challenges. And let him know who the straight shooters are and which ones prefer their advice candy-coated. The precise list differs with each issue, but some essential requirements include:

- The number of participants in your workshop.
- Biographical sketches for each executive.
- Relevant background information on the issues at hand.
- Messages you have developed for your issues (see Chapter Eight for a more detailed discussion of messaging requirements).
- Lists of questions divided into three categories:
  1. Routine questions you expect your spokespeople to receive.
  2. Questions you want reporters to ask them.
  3. Tough questions for which they must be prepared.
- An additional document based on the above questions in a Q&A format that sets forth suggested responses.
- News clips surrounding the issues at hand, particularly any in which your company's spokespeople are quoted.

The above items form the basis of background information upon which your consultant will shape the day's agenda. If you are not able or willing to provide this fundamental information, let him know as soon as possible. The rare times I run into this situation, for example, it tells me that I either need to lower my client's expectations or give them time to locate another person willing to work under such restrictions.

Supplementary Background Information

Most companies should have the above items readily at hand. Digging a level or two deeper, there is other data you can provide your consultant that will facilitate preparation of your workshop and, thereby, raise the odds for a successful experience.

In addition to the above list, consider passing along these items specific to each participant:

- A brief narrative outlining the media experience of each of your C-suite officers. Your workshop leader needs to understand whether they have vast experience or little to none.
- Relevant background information on any competitors or critics. This can take the form of hard copy material, such as annual reports or news clips, or references to online material.
- Any video or audio recordings of media interviews in which your officers have participated. Video or audio of presentations they have delivered can also deliver helpful insights.

Some additional organizational information is also recommended:

- Information on key services or products. This can come in the form of brochures, consumer ads, web pages, and many other modes.
- Information on competitors' services or products.
- Annual/quarterly reports.
- Recent controversies. News clips rarely tell the whole story behind dustups. Offer a brief narrative document that presents additional details and deeper context.
- Challenges, vulnerabilities, and competitive issues that could arise in the form of reporter questions.
- Your website address. While any training consultant worth his salt will long ago have perused your online presence, it is a good idea to provide it regardless. Also, if any of the individual trainees have personal websites, pass along those URLs, too, along with their LinkedIn profiles.
- Competitors' website addresses.
- Recordings of analyst calls, if yours is a public company. These can offer ideas of issues that may arise under questioning from the press.
- List of trade press and reputable blogs that cover your issues. Today's media is fragmented to such a degree, your training consultant may not be familiar with small yet influential outlets that cover your industry.

If your objective is to prepare for an imminent campaign or product launch, be sure to furnish your consultant with a pending media interview schedule or, at the very least, your media targets. As your pitching evolves, update him regularly so he is aware which markets and reporters your executives need to prepare for.

Also send along a copy of your pitch letter and press kit. Remember to update this information as it changes, too. Early on in the process, share drafts of these materials so your consultant has some idea what you want to say and who you want to reach.

Prepare Other Internal Staff

Perhaps the most oft-ignored element of preparing for a media training involves steeling staff members who are not part of the workshop. I can guarantee that your office will be abuzz with chatter about the pending session. Water cooler gossip will range from, "Jim is being dragged to this meeting as punishment for that last lame news interview," to, "Pam gets all the perks. How come they never give us these opportunities?"

I strongly suggest that you nip this gossip in the bud by providing some basic information to everyone. You don't need to unveil the entire strategy, especially if sensitive issues are being discussed. You decide what level of detail is appropriate. But removing some of the mystery allows you to keep a lid on any wild rumors.

Send an office-wide email, post a notice on your intranet, or mention the media training as an agenda item at your staff meeting. Explain that this is all part of your communications plan designed to get your good word out to the public through the press. Don't make an overly big deal about it, but do reach out so that you can preempt some of the tall tales liable to spread through your office if you keep people in the dark.

Minimizing Distractions

A media training workshop is hectic enough on the calmest of days. Refuse to let yours turn into a sideshow that features random staff members traipsing in and out.

Start by restricting the number of people in the training room. Two or three extras is normally the maximum number you will need. Why curb attendance? The more people in the room, the lower the quality of the learning experience for your spokespeople. Discussions get too diffuse and rambling, and the risk of distractions increases exponentially.

Beyond the active participants, one or two people from your communications team should be in the room. These are your in-house message experts (hint: If they are not, get rid of them and hire someone capable).

Next, you must decide, given the specifics of your situation, whether your CEO, president, or vice president overseeing a critical area adds value or not. Also place a limit on the number of issue experts there to aid with factual questions during messaging discussions. It is fine for people to rotate in and out on an as-needed basis, provided you don't turn the session into a never-ending parade.

To avoid lots of noisy coming and going, appoint a "sergeant-at-arms" to monitor those in attendance. If someone strolls in who doesn't belong, gently but firmly escort them out. Your sergeant-at-arms can also assist if side chatter becomes a distraction, though your workshop leader should also be capable of dealing with those types of disruptions.

Given today's business pressures, some individuals in the room may need to deal with other matters on the day of the training. Still, insist that everyone (yes, everyone) turn off their mobile devices when they enter the training sanctum. Show some respect for the learning environment and keep any conversations – either face-to-face or on the telephone – to a minimum and take them out of the room. Also, avoid the temptation to check email. This is highly distracting to everyone in attendance.

It is a good idea to get everyone's assent to your "no interruptions" ground rules at the start of the day. If someone violates those agreed-upon rules, kick them out, no questions asked. I realize that sounds harsh, but it is challenging enough under ideal circumstances to maintain the flow. Even seemingly slight distractions can derail the entire process.

Prepare the Training Facility

The first basic decision you need to make with regard to the training site is where to hold it. Geography certainly plays a role. If, for instance, you need to work with several C-suite officers or board members, the site of your annual meeting or executive retreat may make the most sense. Or your office conference room may be suitable. You can also opt for a hotel function room, conference center, or studio. In fact, if your organization maintains an on-site studio, by all means use it for your media training.

Studios do lend an aura of authority to the proceedings. But a fancy space is not mandatory. Remember that a training consultant who makes a big deal about having a sophisticated studio in his office is building his costs for that facility on the back of your budget. If you want to pay for that overhead, that's fine. You know your needs and financial capabilities best.

Making sure you have the right setup begins with a thorough checklist. Is the training room the right size? Something too big makes the whole process seem insignificant. Something too small feels cramped and creates an inferior learning environment.

Small also hurts because you have some gear that needs to fit. You need either a video monitor or an LCD projector and a screen to allow for video playback. If your workshop leader plans on showing slides during part of a didactic discussion, the projector and screen become mandatory. A flip chart with blank paper or a dry erase board (accompanied by markers that work) is also needed to capture key thoughts.

Beyond the mere size of the room, examine its layout. Are there any support poles or odd corners that could affect seating arrangements or camera angles? Does it front on a noisy street that makes concentration and audio clarity difficult? Will there be a raucous confab featuring a "motivational" sales seminar in the room next door? If you book a function room in a hotel, did they try to stick you in a guest suite (the general layout of these rooms combined with their heavy, immobile furniture makes them notoriously poor options for training workshops)?

Getting the Right Shots

Don't forget to leave some space for the camera and videographer. And yes, you do need a professional videographer. Some organizations try to get by on the cheap by having an inexperienced person videotape the practice exercises. Worse yet, some expect their training consultant to take on that task. The result of this penny-wise yet pound-foolish approach is, sadly, an inferior learning experience. You pay good money for consultants to educate your spokespeople. Don't you deserve 100 percent focus and performance?

Here is what happens when amateurs run the equipment: Video quality suffers due to inferior camera skills and lighting. Audio quality suffers because they try to get by with the sound from the tinny microphone built into their miniature cameras. I witnessed enough of this early in my career and swore, no more.

But here is the real important fact: Workshop leaders who attempt to operate a camera simply face too many distractions, lowering the effectiveness of the learning environment. Any experienced consultant recognizes the need to be able to react quickly to the participants, often changing the "temperature" of the training environment on a moment's notice depending on the signals – both verbal and nonverbal – C-suite members send.

Prepare the Training Agenda

Broken down into its most basic components, most media training workshops feature three areas: 1) Establishing a baseline of understanding; 2) Message development; and 3) experiential simulations.

Some consultants prefer to begin every session with a review of media relations basics, then lump all the practice interviews into whatever time is left at the end of the schedule. That may work in some cases, but I suggest avoiding this one-size-fits-all approach.

The key to setting the agenda is to determine what is proper for the participants. You should sketch out a blueprint with your consultant as part of your preparation phase. Do keep in mind that he should be skilled at reading what the participants need as the day progresses. If he decides to change something on the fly, there is likely a compelling educational reason for doing so.

My clients sometimes ask me for a training agenda very early in the preparation process. Honestly, I have no idea what to tell them until I become more familiar with the needs of their C-suite and their business. I freely admit that, if pressed, I will send them a sample agenda just to help them attain a comfort level. But that piece of paper usually bears little resemblance to the final curriculum.

Didactic portions of the training can range from a Media 101 approach for those unschooled at dealing with reporters to a quick brush up for those accustomed to being interviewed.

It bears repeating that this discussion does not need to occur in isolation at the beginning of your workshop. In fact, I contend that learners are much more receptive to certain advice as situations arise as part of the process. If, for instance, your chief technology officer tends to repeat negative language put forth by the reporter, her mind is much more attuned to a learning moment after she has viewed herself on video repeating a negative. It may blow right by her if presented during a windy introductory lecture.

The questionnaire outlined earlier should reveal to some degree the experience of the learners. You and your consultant also need to do some independent digging. Plug their names into your favorite search engine to see what pops up. Poke around digital media sites like LinkedIn, Twitter, and YouTube to see what type of online trail they have left. If the company is publicly traded, sources like *The Wall Street Journal* can offer valuable insights.

Message Development

Beware. Message development is the one area where most media trainings fall apart. Some organizations do take messaging seriously and have crafted magnetic messages. In my experience, however, they are a distinct minority. Sadly, this same truth exists if you employ a public relations or public affairs agency to help with message development. Some are quite skilled, but too many fail to grasp the difference between airtight messaging and a laundry list of disjointed bullet points.

You have a choice regarding message development. Option one involves hammering out your messages in advance of the workshop. This is by far the most effective approach for it allows your trainees to begin to internalize the material before the practice interviews take place.

It is important that you share your messages with your workshop leader as soon as practical. I like to get them from my clients early in the planning process, even if in draft form. Odds are there is no one on your staff as experienced at message development as a veteran communications strategy consultant. You are paying good money for that service. Get all you can from it by asking your consultant to review your messages. He may have suggestions ranging from a quick tweak to a total overhaul depending on the thoroughness of your work.

Try not to take these suggestions personally. They should be made with your long-term business goals in mind. If you disagree with anything, speak up. Explain why you organized it the way you did or why it is important to say something exactly as you wrote it. You have day-to-day context that your consultant lacks.

That's one reason why it's a best practice for an internal communications staffer to sit in on the training workshop. It also does you some good when the consultant makes you an active part of the session, drawing you into discussions and soliciting your feedback. This not only adds to the quality of the learning experience, it boosts your credibility with your C-suite. Plus, in future discussions, you are in position to remind them what your consultant advised and how to follow through.

Expect the messages you begin with to change during the workshop based on feedback from your C-suite. This is altogether normal and to be expected, for a message is an always-evolving creature. Perhaps one leg of your message falls apart under intense questioning during a practice interview. That is a positive development. Better for that to occur in the security of your workshop than in a high-stakes interview with a key reporter.

Option two is to create messages during your media training. Just understand that this will result in a lengthier session and stands to drain time from the experiential portion of the training. One way around this is to call in your consultant to lead a separate messaging session before your training occurs. Just be sure to label it a messaging session – not a media training – so that everyone involved has a clear understanding of the task at hand.

Remain open to sensible changes as you go through the messaging process. It is a dynamic procedure. Nothing is ever etched in stone.

Experiential Exercises

All simulations – or practice interviews – should be recorded to video. This applies even if your executives are not expected to appear on television. Why? Viewing and critiquing the video immediately after the fact represents the most powerful learning moments participants are likely to encounter.

Even print reporters are watching for subtle (and not so subtle, for that matter) nonverbal signals. A video critique demonstrates vividly body language pluses and minuses. And remember to insist on a professional videographer to capture the interviews.

Your consultant should ask about the types of interview situations the participants are likely to face. If he fails to ask, tell him. Effective simulations involve more than simply trotting your executives willy-nilly in front of a camera.

Setting up a practice interview for a satellite media tour opportunity, for example, involves different parameters than a telephone interview by a print reporter or a podcast. Your training consultant and videographer need to be adept at creating as closely as possible the atmosphere of the real thing.

They may need to shift the set between interviews. If your consultant has properly briefed the videographer, these transitions should be seamless, with the videographer handling the physical set changes while the workshop leader continues the education process.

Post-session Agenda

Neglect the value of post-session feedback at your company's peril. Remember, this is not a one-off proposition. Rather, it is a single step in your C-suite's professional development.

I admit to being stubborn about this, but I have witnessed too many organizations content to say their spokespeople have been "media trained" just because they have gone through one session.

Smart businesses comprehend the learning continuum and embrace it. Assuming you fall into that category, be sure to ask your consultant about his commitment to sustained learning at the very beginning of your professional relationship. Does he offer post-training consultation via telephone or email? A written report? Follow-up workshops? What lifelong learning materials does he leave with his students?

Presuming your consultant is a thought leader in his field, does he leave trainees with a copy of his book or training guide? (Note: Ask some detailed questions about the materials he offers. Some organizations will settle for a handful of quick copied sheets stapled together; others prefer a publication that can advance learning in stages over time).

Some consultants, as part of their professional fee, even offer articles you can run in your publications. This advances the learning not only of those in the room during the training, but throughout your organization as well.

Your C-suite's Success Formula

Rewarding professional development programs are designed by choice, not by chance. Keep yourself on the right path by doing your homework ahead of time:

- Prepare your C-suite participants.
- Prepare your training consultant.
- Prepare other internal staff.
- Prepare the training facility.
- Prepare the program agenda.

Following these best practice standards leads to more than a successful professional development experience for your C-suite. Bear in mind the words of Nelson Mandela: "Education is the most powerful weapon which you can use to change the world" – or in this case, the minds of your target audience. This ongoing commitment leads to achievement of your organization's goals – from a healthier bottom line to public policy success, from greater career opportunities to an ability to outperform the competition.

Those larger goals are what your professional development efforts are all about. What happens when things are left to chance? Read on.

Five for the Future

Chapter Seven dealt with the value of communications training for media outreach, public speaking campaigns, and advocacy efforts. Consider what you need to know to implement a long-term influencer training program for your C-suite. Use these "Five for the Future" discussion questions to help you sustain your C-suite's professional development over the long run. Discuss these issues with co-workers, professional colleagues, mentors, and in your own mind:

1. How can you move from a "one and done" mindset to one that views communications training workshops as but one step in improving your company's communications abilities?
2. How much, if any, of this training can you handle internally?
3. Under what circumstances do you need to call in an experienced consultant who knows the training game inside and out?
4. How can you persuade reluctant C-suiters that they should participate in a media training workshop?

5.   What videos can you show your C-suite to drive home your points about the value of communications training?

Bonus content

You may need media, presentation skills, or legislative testimony training. Looking for some solid advice to help ramp up your capabilities? Log on to www.barkscomm.com/APlusBonus for your copy of "The Basics of Communications."

CHAPTER 8

MESSAGING

Consider your business and public policy goals. No matter how lofty or practical they may be, the central question becomes, how do you achieve them? Says author J.K. Rowling, "We do not need magic to change the world, we carry all the power we need inside ourselves already. We have the power to imagine better."

Sorry to tell you there is no easy, one-size-fits-all messaging solution. It's challenging work that smart companies undertake.

Get ready, for we're about to lay out a system featuring 11 elements that will get you started. Some of these 11 elements to elicit a magnetic message are universal. Others may apply only in certain circumstances. It's up to your communications team, top executives, and the expert consultants you utilize to implement these steps correctly.

Here are some points to keep in mind as you craft your message. What is the best format to deliver the word? You may find it helpful to explain it through a number of different means. For instance, would you be wise to create visuals like charts? Even the font you use matters; a playful typeface would be inappropriate if you are discussing a dread disease. Perhaps you want to demonstrate your innovation via video or audio channels.

Maybe it makes sense to send your executives out on the hustings to tout the good word. Or you may choose to draft a series of articles for placement in pivotal publications. A radio talk show or podcast campaign may be advisable.

What about the tone – are you aiming for hopeful or do you need to talk about a serious situation? Also contemplate the context in which you're operating. If you are announcing quarterly financials on a day when the stock markets are in free fall, you'd best be ready for some serious probing from the financial community and the journalists who cover it. Timing also comes into play. There's a reason you can buy Halloween candy for pennies on the dollar on November 1.

As noted elsewhere, repetition is a good thing as you hammer home your message. You should be shouting the same words from every rooftop. This applies not only to individual presentations and media interviews, but to the channels you utilize to reinforce your news. You can repeat essentially the same message in your C-suite speeches, your company's blog and digital media accounts, your encounters with reporters, and your in-house newsletter.

What are those 11 elements that can help you fortify your message development and delivery capabilities? Let's examine each so you can begin to implement this system right away.

1. Identify

A magnetic message requires, first and foremost, a target audience. Identify those groups and individuals you need to reach and aim your communication toward them. Of course, this target is likely to change from issue to issue. For example, your company may plan release of a new product today while confronting a thorny public policy issue tomorrow. The upshot? Be sure to identify your prime audiences for each message you shape.

Address your audience with a foundation of four strong points – or legs. These are the main tenets you want to convey in your presentations, during your media interviews, and when visiting your elected officials.

Others may have advised you that a message consists of three points. I began to question that construct. My intuition told me that three is too limiting, so I kept asking those who insisted on three being the magic number why – why three main points? Where's the proof? What research can you show to back up that contention? I never got a satisfactory answer. Then, a few years ago I came across findings from Nelson Cowan, University of Missouri Professor of Psychology. In brief, he held that the number of items one can hold in mind is four, assuming the thoughts aren't overly complex.

That's why you should think of your message as a sturdy, four-legged chair. If one of the chair legs is weak, it collapses, sending you crashing to the floor. So it is with your message. One weak point, and your communications efforts fall in a heap.

There is no single correct way to shape a message. How you go about it depends on your situation and the issue at hand. Some examples of messaging methodology include:

- The classic problem/solution/next step formulation. What is the missing fourth leg here? Context, a crucial point discussed in greater detail in just a moment.
- Chronological. Start with context, then describe yesterday, today, and tomorrow.
- Informational, when you don't need to persuade, merely to educate.
- Adversarial, when someone picks a fight with you and you need to strike back (verbally, of course).

The fact is many companies neglect to create formal messages tailored to their key constituencies. Or if they do, the messaging is sometimes weak. Experience shows that the size of the organization makes little difference. I have worked with smaller organizations possessing well-crafted messages and with Fortune 500 companies (and, sad to say, sometimes their public relations agencies) who either have not thought things through properly or who are ignorant in message development techniques, resulting in abysmal communication with key groups.

If you don't want to see your message flatlining like an unfortunate patient on Grey's Anatomy, it is imperative to consider both internal and external stakeholders, too. For example, if you work in a pharmaceutical firm touting a new drug, what do diverse audiences like physicians, patient advocacy groups, insurance companies, regulators, the media, suppliers, labor unions, rivals, market analysts, pharmacists, your employees, and hospital administrators think? Do some of them hold similar interests? Where is there a divergence of opinion? While your message needs to remain consistent across all of your target audiences, which part of your message you emphasize may vary.

2. Construct

Just as there are many ways to create a great tasting recipe, there is no universal best way to cook up a magnetic message. You need an internal communications staff or an external consultant experienced in message development to lead your company through the process.

That said, the fact is many an organization's messages lack two important legs. The first is context. We all tend to take our issues for granted since we deal with them day in and day out. Your target audience knows far less, so offer a baseline to help them understand.

The other overlooked ingredient involves next steps. What do you expect your audience to do with your message? What call to action are you issuing? Unless your message is purely informational (a rarity), explain what you want them to do after consuming your quotes in a news article or listening to your speech.

Additionally, keep out any jargon or technobabble. As author A.A. Milne advised, "It is more fun to talk with someone who doesn't use long, difficult words but rather short, easy words, like 'What about lunch?'"

3. Collaborate

Pay attention to who's in the room during your message development sessions. The composition of your team is likely to change for each issue. Some groups, for example, may include the CEO, regional vice presidents, issue experts, lawyers, communications staff, and relevant consultants. Other teams may involve just a few of these people or include those from other disciplines.

The important consideration is that everyone with a stake or special expertise needs to be there. Of equal importance, anyone superfluous to the issue should be barred from the room. This helps you avoid too unwieldy a process.

Also, keep the sycophants away. You need executives and experts willing to lay their ideas on the line. As famed Hollywood producer Samuel Goldwyn said, "I don't want yes-men around me. I want everyone to tell the truth, even if it costs them their jobs."

4. Focus

There are no shortcuts to developing a magnetic message. Indeed, message development workshops can often be sweat-producing, heart-pounding, headache-inducing affairs.

You won't necessarily see fireworks and hear shouting (though some sessions can be intense). Still, honest and civil dissent should be viewed as productive.

To begin the process, devote some time to brainstorming or brainwriting. Make sure to commit your ideas to paper, so nothing gets lost in what is often a hectic procedure with ideas flying fast and furious.

To smooth out the process, choose a facilitator who can remain impartial in guiding your deliberations. This person could be someone inside your organization who has no stake in the issue at hand or an outsider. Just be sure she understands and agrees that her role is solely to move the process forward, not to take part in substantive discussions.

5. Examine

Here's a quick review of some of the questions you'll need to address as you craft your message:

- Who is my audience?
- What are my goals and objectives for this campaign, issue, or crisis?
- What is the audience's current perspective and baseline of information?
- What matters to my audience and what benefits can they expect?
- What do they care about on an emotional level, and how can I connect with that?
- What do I want them to support, condemn, or take action upon?
- What is likely to motivate them to take action?
- Where are my vulnerabilities?
- Where is my data or proof weak, making me subject to attack?
- Which are the most concrete proof points I can offer?
- What inherent strengths does my company possess?
- What facets of my personal background give me an edge in their eyes?
- What makes my contention better than my opposition's?
- What is the single best quotable quote I want them to recall and re-state?
- How can I best transform them into disciples of my message?
- What "call to action" must I sound?

You'll probably be able to ignore some of these questions depending on your situation. And you will no doubt explore additional questions specific to your issue or industry. The important point is to unearth the concerns that put you on the fast lane of the messaging highway.

6. Flavor

The spoken word must contain some spice, so salt the four legs of your message with some quotable quotes. When skeptics say, "Prove it," your quotes need to do just that while adding some punch to your delivery.

Here is a list of some of the tools you have at your fingertips:

- Stories - Telling a memorable tale makes your message more impressive.
- Numbers - Help your listeners size up your message with mental pictures of millions, dozens, fractions, and percentages.

- Vivid Words - Color your language with action words and phrases your audience will store in their mind's scrapbook.
- Analogies - Bring clear pictures to the mind's eye with these comparisons.
- Extremes - Tell your listeners that you are the first, the best, or the only (and of experiences you've had with the last or the worst).
- Case studies - Mention true to life situations that have affected you and your business.
- Third-party endorsements - Offer praise from famous names and delighted clients.
- Topics du jour - Sprinkle your conversation with references to current events and the latest in movies, TV, music, and sports.
- Famous quotes - Use words of wisdom from those you admire.
- Ju Jitsu - Cite your rivals when they speak favorably of you.
- Surveys - Demonstrate why public opinion is on your side.
- Research reports - Support your contentions with solid proof backed by your own research.
- Calls to action - Urge readers and viewers to call your office, visit your website, or write their member of Congress.
- Best case/worst case scenarios - Provide a glimpse into the future.
- Comparisons - How is your stance superior to that of your rival?
- Photographs - What's that old saw about a picture being worth a thousand words?
- Video - If a picture is worth a thousand words, what do you imagine video is worth?
- Charts and graphs - Don't go overboard with the data, but simple, elegant graphics can sometimes prove your point.
- Humor - It not likely you are a stand-up comedian, though situational humor can help loosen things up.
- Clichés - Used judiciously, these can resonate.
- Demonstrations of your product or service - The proof is in the pudding (and if you're a pudding maker, give yourself a few bonus points).

7. Fortify

There is no substitute for ongoing practice. Just as baseball players take swings in the batting cage before every game, the best media interview subjects, public speakers, and Congressional witnesses take practice seriously.

This preparation needs to occur both formally and informally. On a formal level, schedule regular communications training sessions with all of your spokespeople. Discuss your messaging to ensure they have internalized it. Then conduct a few practice rounds to confirm they can verbalize it. Your internal staff (assuming they have the wherewithal) can handle some of these sessions, though it is helpful to bring in an experienced communications training consultant on critical issues and for the occasional tune up.

Informally, look for pop-up practice opportunities. You don't always need to devote the hours it takes to hold a formal training workshop. For instance, take those 10 minutes between meetings to review your message or develop a quotable quote for it. Toss questions at one another during random encounters around the water cooler. Develop quick-hitting scenarios you can accomplish via email. For instance, pretend a reporter just called with a tough question; how would you use your message to respond?

The confidence gained during such exercises will help put some steel in your executives' spines when it comes to broadcasting your message during media interviews, presentations, and exchanges with elected officials.

8. Heed

I guarantee this will happen at some point. It's human nature to tune out the familiar every now and again.

Internal experts lose their sway at times. Don't worry. It's probably not you. It's not your executives. It just happens over time. Being a prophet in your own land does have its drawbacks. How to handle this diminishing return?

I can best illustrate by sharing a story from my time in the association realm some years ago. We produced an internal media training program for our officers and other key members to help them better understand our organizational messages and to polish their communications skills. It was well received and empowered the organization with a more elegant and disciplined approach to media outreach. Nonetheless, at least once annually we brought in veteran media training consultants.

Why did we do this, given the success of our internal program? We found that a different voice – not necessarily better or worse, just different – helped our leaders grow as communicators. As an added benefit, when we needed to rein someone in, the consultant could frame things in terms more stark than we could (I did want to keep my job, after all). We had frank conversations with our consultants during the preparation phase, discussing what issues needed to be placed on the table and how we expected them to address those matters.

9. Test

Once you have achieved a first cut of your magnetic message, it is time to see if it can withstand rigorous questioning. What is the best way to test its attraction? Think of all the tough questions reporters, audience members, and public officials could toss at you. If your message responds successfully, you are in good shape.

It is vital that your preparations include practice dealing with hardballs. Going over questions in your mind is not enough. Simulate the real thing by having co-workers give you the third degree. Make the office skeptic a part of your routine (for a wonderful treatment of why you need these folks involved, I highly recommend *In Defense of Troublemakers* by Charlan Nemeth). If one or more of your message points is responsive to the salvos of this cynic, you likely have attained the necessary magnetism.

Another method of testing your message is to seek reaction from trusted colleagues and peers outside your organization. This external criticism can provide you with the unvarnished insights you need before venturing into the real world.

For higher stakes opportunities, you may wish to consider more formal measurements, such as surveying key constituencies.

10. Chronicle

Put your messages in writing. Never skip this step even when the issue seems fairly minor. This will aid greatly with your company's message discipline and consistency. Keep it simple. There's no need to waste time and energy doodling with an overly complicated diagram or trendy infographic (of course, it's fine to develop such tools for outreach purposes after you've ascertained that your message is ready for prime time).

Stick to a one-page document that highlights the four legs of your message. Below each main point, include bullet points that support your contentions and suggest quotable quotes, using the techniques outlined above. Sticking to this one-page format also helps you keep things streamlined, automatically instilling discipline that helps you avoid the verbal excess that afflicts so many organizations.

Revisit your message regularly, for it is a constantly evolving creature. There is no guarantee that today's magnetic message will suffice tomorrow, so reexamine your message on a quarterly basis at a minimum, more often for rapidly shifting issues. The frequency depends on such factors as how swiftly your environment changes, the profile of the issue, and changes in your C-suite team or spokesperson roster.

11. Broadcast

You have a toolkit full of useful instruments available to you when getting your message out to the media, to target audiences, and to policymakers. Some fit in certain situations and not in others, so make some conscious decisions about what makes sense when. This list is by no means exhaustive, though it gives you a good starting point:

- Media interviews.
- Speeches to industry conferences.
- Presentations to clients and prospective clients.
- Congressional testimony.
- Fly-in visits with members of Congress.
- Digital media tools like Facebook, Instagram, and Twitter.
- News releases.
- Written statements on breaking issues.
- Editorial board visits.
- Satellite media tours.
- News conferences.
- Your website.
- Guest articles and op-eds for newspapers and trade publications.
- Newsletters.
- One-sheet leave behind for elected officials.
- Organizational blogs.
- Webinars.

Is Your Message Missing Its Call to Action?

Let's dig deeper into the all-too-frequently missing call to action. A recent paper in the *Stanford Social Innovation Review* titled "Stop Raising Awareness Already" supports a principle I've long been driving home to my clients: Most messaging lacks a clear call to action.

The paper's authors, Ann Christiano and Annie Neimand, both of the University of Florida College of Journalism and Communications, argue that raising the public's level of awareness isn't enough. They write that activists – and I would include corporate and association executives in the mix, too – should "craft campaigns that use messaging and concrete calls to action that get people to change how they feel, think, or act, and as a result create long-lasting change."

Some clients look somewhat shaken when I tell them that public information campaigns, while noble, are in many cases a colossal waste of time and resources, both human and capital. You've educated people. Great. Now what? How does a more informed public help your organization's cause? Are they buying your product or contributing to your cause? Are they voting the way you want? Hmm, not so much, eh?

In their paper, Christiano and Neimand note, "Research and experience both show that we must define actionable and achievable calls to action that will lead a specific group of people to do something they haven't done before."

Strategic communications training is more than teaching executives to talk pretty. The ultimate aim is to help a business reach its goals and to help participants enhance their career paths. Part of reaching both of those objectives means empowering them with a clear and powerful call to action. Otherwise, they are indeed doing little more than learning to talk pretty.

What's more, this call to action needs to be meaningful. Going forth with a limp message that just preaches to the choir does no one any good. If your motivation consists of boosting your Facebook likes or Twitter followers, you're not persuading anyone. You're just making yourself feel better while basking in the comfort of your private echo chamber.

Recall our scheme for political operatives covered in Chapter Five. A quick and dirty means of measuring support for a candidate is to rank voters from 1 to 5. The 1s are with you no matter what; the 5s will fight you to the death. Smart campaigns all but ignore both ends of the spectrum and concentrate on the 3s – those who are sitting on the fence. So it should be with any corporate messaging campaign. Persuade those who need persuasion and who may be open to it.

What might such calls to actions involve? Consider the following forums:

- Presentations: What do you want audience members buzzing about in the corridors after your talk?
- Media interviews: What do you want the reporter to write?
- Public policy initiatives: How do you want that lawmaker to vote?

As Christiano and Neimand write, one risk "that poorly devised awareness campaigns have is that they reach a different audience than the one that was intended. This might be an audience that is unsympathetic to the campaign's goals or one that might already be convinced of its goals."

They go on to say, "There are four essential elements to creating a successful public interest communications campaign: target your audience as narrowly as possible; create compelling messages with clear calls to action; develop a theory of change; and use the right messenger."

The next time you caucus for a message development session or communications training workshop, make sure to put these questions on the table: What is their perspective on our position? How can we align our "asks" with their interests? What do we want our target audiences to do once they understand our stance? How can we lead them there?

When the Tectonic Plates Jolt You into a New Reality

It's never a good thing when companies express uncertainty. One of the prime examples of late was the corporate jitteriness in the wake of the 2016 presidential election results.

Most businesses and associations felt relatively comfortable with their reach into the Hillary Clinton transition team (with the exception, of course, of those interests diametrically opposed to what she stands for; yet even there, familiarity provided some degree of solace since unpredictability can cause more stress than outright opposition). Donald Trump's election upset the apple cart to an unimaginable extent. Few organizations had deep ties to team Trump. Add to that the president-elect's mercurial nature, and even those of his own party were flummoxed.

This high level of uncertainty got me to thinking of ways of overcoming – or at least assuaging somewhat – that uncertainty. For one, I rounded up an informal group of fellow Beltway insiders to compare notes on who's who in the coming administration. Some of the big names had been announced. But the rubber really hits the road when appointments for deputies, undersecretaries, and the like begin. Those are the individuals who will sort through and, in many cases, decide the nuts and bolts of new laws and regulations.

What does that mean to businesses with public policy interests? The fun had just begun. Unless they already had an "in" with the cabinet secretary overseeing their interests, we advised them to heed the thousands of lower level federal appointments. Collectively, we kept a finger on this pulse as a service to our clients.

The second front involved what in many cases was a reconfiguring of public policy messages. We pointed out that government affairs staffs, aided by communications teams, should be giving code red priority to this effort. The cruel fact is many organizations don't have the horsepower to get the job done quickly, successfully, and correctly.

How could companies go about assessing capabilities in the face of a new political environment? We suggested a few messaging options:

- Add in extra context to your messages. It is important to bear in mind that many of the new government officials would have little if any government experience. That matters. A lot. Government cannot be run like a business. Sure, certain principles may be useful.

But government exists to do things the private sector cannot or will not do.

- Educate the new arrivals. They have probably never run anything as large and complex as a government bureaucracy (a word I use with no malintent). They may have little understanding of the fact that they will have 535 overseers on Capitol Hill, each with their own fiefdom and each of whom is likely to be thoroughly unimpressed with another deputy underassistant secretary.

- The duck and cover approach. Some businesses had already adopted this method, doing their best not to enter the president-elect's line of sight. Do you think it's fun or profitable to be the target of a nasty tweet? We noted that the CEO of Boeing learned this the hard way.

- Reassess your legislative and regulatory goals. The landscape changed dramatically. Those who thought they had a good plan of attack with a Clinton administration were stuck with no battle plan and no ammunition. If their views were more friendly to the incoming crew, was it wise to make more aggressive asks? If the corporation was on the losing side, should they pare back their public policy goals?

- Crisis planning. One vivid example here: How could green organizations (anything from the Sierra Club to a large corporation that has seen the wisdom and business benefits of going green) counter an inevitable attack from an Environmental Protection Agency nominee who not only opposes your viewpoint, but denies problems even exist?

- Attitude adjustment. Internally, some firms may need to recalibrate their advocates and their workforce in order to lessen the odds of an organization-wide depression. What message should they send to their own troops?

- Keep things the same. Burying your head in the sand will do you no good (unless you happen to represent an association of ostriches).

These are but a few of the possible methods for messaging in new times. The hard truth is, when the landscape tilts rapidly and unexpectedly, you need experts capable of shaping your messages quickly, successfully, and correctly.

The Bottom Line

Your company's reputation is next to impossible to rehabilitate, once tarnished. Shoddy messaging is one surefire way to sully that reputation.

Let your competitors be the ones who deliver those embarrassing presentations, spew mealy-mouthed quotes to the press, and undermine their encounters with policymakers.

Crafting a magnetic message with four strong legs, holding a workshop to ensure you've got it right, involving the right people in its development, and bringing on board an expert consultant for critical issues goes a long way toward gaining victory for your company.

Also, don't forget to instill your C-suite with the discipline to deliver your message, road test it, and commit it to writing.

Follow these common sense guidelines. They can help your company raise the odds of achieving your long-term business goals and public policy objectives. Your reputation hangs in the balance.

Five for the Future

A magnetic message is critical to your company's success, as demonstrated in Chapter Eight. Use these "Five for the Future" discussion questions to help you sustain your messaging efforts and your C-suite's influence over the long haul. Discuss these issues with co-workers, professional colleagues, mentors, and in your own mind:

1. If your company has neglected to shape cohesive messaging one-pagers, how can you make it happen?
2. How often should you review your messaging on issues that are vital to your bottom line success?
3. Of the 11 elements that go into crafting a magnetic message, where do you need the most help?
4. Look at your current messaging. Have you provided context for your target audience? What about a call to action?
5. Do you have all the knowledge you need to develop magnetic messaging, or do you need to call in an experienced consultant?

Bonus content

Your message needs to be dressed up with quotable quotes. Yet there are trite phrases sure to backfire. Learn what they are and how to avoid them by downloading your copy of "Magnetizing Your Message" at www.barkscomm.com/APlusBonus.

CHAPTER 9

REPUTATIONAL RISK

The day started innocently enough. I went online to pay some bills, yet was unable to log into my bank account. The message on the screen warned me that the connection could not be made for security reasons.

It was then that I noticed the alert on the bank's home page. Its system refused to work with the latest version of the Firefox browser update. Apparently, my online banking service was taken by surprise by an entirely predictable occurrence.

I tried two points of contact with the bank. First, I sent an email to the customer service address provided on the website. I waited nearly 12 hours for a reply. When it became clear that responsive customer service meant something different to them than to me, I picked up the phone. A defensive operator informed me that it would take two weeks for their technology vendor to solve the problem, and that there was no one else I could talk to about this.

Reputational Risk Affects Profits

I should note that this small community bank has received the bulk of my personal and commercial business for decades. It is comforting to be called by name when doing business there. Unfortunately, this was one of those times when an evolving business environment dictated a larger and more competent IT capability.

All things considered, I'll probably keep some accounts at the bank in question. However, after many years of turning to it without question, I'll now think twice before placing any new business there.

The top priority when planning for a potential crisis is to do the right thing in the first place. In this case, the bank would have been wise to communicate an intent to beef up its technology capabilities going forward and inform customers what to expect.

This was a crisis that should have been foreseen. To be sure, technology must change to keep pace with the black hats. Yet browser updates are common occurrences. No reputable bank, and certainly not its IT firm, should be caught with its drawers down. Tellingly, I encountered no other website that was similarly affected, which leads me to think they need to review their vendor.

Someone at the bank should have played skeptic and asked how such an update would affect their customers' browsing habits (and, of course, it was the vendor's responsibility to test the new system on all possible software). Gaming out how the bank might respond to reputational risk situations like this might have saved them some customers.

The fact that this bank has been heavily involved in its community for years stood to its benefit. It took an extroverted approach to its reputation. Introverted firms, as labeled by Charles Fombrun in his book *Reputation: Realizing Value from the Corporate Image,* are liable to have a harder time recovering from reputational dings. Why? When companies lay low and eschew cultivating an image of any sort, the first impression the public has is negative. The business has no reputational capital in its bank.

It would be wise to assess where your company is on the extroversion/introversion scale, the plan accordingly should your reputation fall under siege.

Threat Assessment

Reputational risk is regarded as the greatest threat to a company's market value, according to a 2004 study by PricewaterhouseCoopers and the Economist Intelligence Unit, as reported by *Canadian Underwriter.*

In addition, reputational risk is the toughest menace of all to handle according to 92 percent of companies, reports *Insurance Journal* in an article published July 23, 2013.

This begs the question, what do you need to do to avoid or, at least, minimize the reputational risk to your business? We'll examine a series of reputational risk scenarios in this chapter designed to help you navigate those hazards.

Before doing so, some background. Managing reputational risk has become an essential leadership skill for executives. Superb performance in this area presents opportunity for C-suite inhabitants and chief communicators to earn their stripes. Indeed, some analysts have suggested that CEO pay be tied to reputation management.

Why not? Consensus dictates that finance, marketing, manufacturing, and personnel all need to be managed. Doesn't that priceless asset – reputation – merit the same treatment?

Goldman Sachs lists its business principles on its website, and reputation is prominently featured: "Our assets are our people, capital and reputation. If any of these is ever diminished, the last is the most difficult to restore." Bear in mind this comes from money people.

Publications like *Bloomberg Businessweek* and *Fortune* publish lists of most admired companies. It may be worth your while to examine what and who they measure, and how those benchmarks apply to your business. Such research might give you ideas of how you can boost your firm's reputation.

Then there is the familiar refrain, "It's not what you know, it's who you know." I suggest this phrase is no longer operational. Today's meme is "It's not who you know, it's who knows you and what they know about you."

What Is Reputational Risk, Anyway?

While there is no single consensus definition of the term "reputational risk," most attempts point in the same general direction. Marsh LLC and Oliver Wyman define it as follows: "Everything an organization does or says creates an indelible impression in the minds of its key stakeholders – senior management, employees, customers, local communities, investors, and so on. The sum total of all these interactions represents your reputation." (*Reputation Risk: A Rising C-Suite Imperative*, 2014, Oliver Wyman).

Here's how the Federal Reserve System's Commercial Bank Examination Manual defines it: "The potential that negative publicity regarding an institution's business practices, whether true or not, will cause a decline in the customer base, costly litigation or revenue reductions."

British management consultant John Elkington suggests that companies consider three bottom lines: financial, environmental, and social performance. All are unquestionably important facets of any business. Yet it seems incomplete.

Introducing the Fourfold Bottom Line

Thus, I recommend making "Reputation" part of a new construct, the Fourfold Bottom Line, if you will (with proper credit to Elkington for building upon his original concept).

One supplement to these recommendations, and one more step in implementing a Fourfold Bottom Line: It is worth reiterating that dealing effectively with reputational risk involves not only preparing for potential crises, but also assessing performance once your reputational crisis subsides. That after action review is a mandatory component.

When your reputation gets dinged, you need to know how to respond. That's why this chapter contains step-by-step procedures and resources to help you counter a variety of risk scenarios.

Firefighters, hospital workers, pilots, and police officers all train rigorously for potential calamities. Corporate executives must, too. Workers from the C-suite to the tiniest cubicles need to be vested in your company's reputation. Your top brass, communications staff, lawyers, and issue experts have a responsibility – financial and ethical – to communicate effectively when catastrophe strikes. The situation may be foreseen or unforeseen, natural or human-made, relatively mild or thoroughly earth-shattering.

One thing to bear in mind: Your voyage to a sparkling reputation can be a Christopher Columbus-like expedition, demanding years of yeoman's work and much uncertainty along the way.

One important factor to make clear to your C-suite: You don't necessarily assess risk to expunge it; that is difficult to impossible. Rather, you examine it to be aware of its impact, breadth, intensity, and probability. This conversation with your leadership can be a difficult one. They sometimes labor under the impression that the communications staff can snap its fingers and make the day sunny and bright. You and I know that's not the real world. Nonetheless, it's your job to help them arrive at this realization.

Impress upon them the benefits your company receives thanks to a positive reputation. People are more likely to give your new product or service a chance, pay more for it, believe your ads, apply for a job in your firm, join your public policy campaigns, purchase your stock, and support you when the waters get choppy.

Prepare for Code Red

Companies that manage reputational threats sufficiently prepare as best they can and assess their performance afterward in an effort to improve future performance. Leadership takes seriously the need for preparation and review to manage shocks to their reputation's system.

Smart businesses take a comprehensive approach to risk management, taking into account various risks including strategic, public policy, operational, financial, and legal. Keeping these functions trapped in silos does no one any good.

Any worthwhile crisis expert will tell you that no one is capable of accurately anticipating the precise predicaments you might face. There are simply too many moving parts. It is akin to playing the stock market; as

John Maynard Keynes held, "Successful investing is anticipating the anticipations of others."

Like the airline pilot who doesn't know if he'll encounter clear air turbulence, an engine flame-out, or a flock of birds, he must be prepared to react to something unexpected at that exact moment in time. So it is with any blows your reputation may suffer, worthy of a tweet storm or not. You must be ready to analyze your situation carefully. An incident that has little impact on one corporation could represent a full-blown reputational crisis for another.

Fully 81 percent of companies view reputation as their number one asset according to a July 23, 2013, *Reuters* account of the report "Reputation at Risk," issued by the insurer ACE. Executives at these companies also concede that they find reputational risk tricky to manage.

In the survey, 77 percent of companies found it problematic to evaluate the financial impact of reputational risk on their business. Sixty-eight percent found it difficult to locate advice about managing reputational risk.

Still, there is hope that smart companies are beginning to see a link between risk management and development of business strategy. As one respondent to the Marsh/RIMS study "Organizational Dynamics: A Focus for Effective Risk Management" noted, "There is significantly more interest, buy-in, and enthusiasm from our executives about looking at strategic risk rather than just operational or financial business risk."

Another participant said, "I wish there were some way we could measure success by thought leadership or by the value we bring to our business partners," adding in a burst of candor, "But I can't figure out a metric for that."

State regulators are also weighing in. In a May 2018 skirmish over insurance provided by the National Rifle Association, New York State financial regulators made clear their role "is to supervise regulated entities to mitigate the risks, 'including reputational risk'" according to *The Wall Street Journal.*

I'm no accountant, but in light of this consideration by financial regulators, I can't help but wonder if reputational risk will one day appear on a firm's balance sheet.

Your C-suite Must Get Engaged

Given this added regulatory scrutiny, it is imperative for your CEO, chair of the board, and the board as a whole to assume responsibility for the company's reputation. Smart organizations know that their board is a decision-making body. A board meeting is not a place to review how wonderful (or how awful) things are. A well-functioning board's agenda needs to look forward, holding regular reviews of matters that could affect the business in the future. Any proposal put before the board should contain an analysis of the impact on your reputation. Your chief reputation officer should vet any such proposal before board members see it.

These leaders need to insist that your chief reputation officer – whatever that person's title (e.g., vice president of communications, public affairs director) – participates in policy decisions. The latter's role needs to be strategic, not a merely tactical function of pitching reporters and lining up speaking engagements for the C-suite.

Fombrun believes that a good chief reputation officer assesses such issues as potential bumps in the road; your company's ability to anticipate such factors as rogue behavior, ethical lapses, and dirty linen; your ability to respond to unforeseen events; and the monitoring systems implemented in attempts to short circuit any crises.

Why place a communications expert in such a critical role? They bear responsibility for messaging that connects not only with the media, but with shareholders, trade associations, members, academics, vendors, government officials, advocacy groups, and more. They need to know how to develop and communicate a broad view of the business. Sure, financial and legal employees may have a similarly broad view, but they often lack a sensitivity to how words will land with the public. Human resource workers are focused internally, so they are poor candidates. Marketing is also a mistake since it concentrates narrowly on moving products or services.

Minimizing Your Reputational Risk

What steps can help you lessen your risk? Inoculate your organization by broadcasting positive news regularly via a variety of channels. Traditional outlets like print and broadcast media, and speeches by your executives qualify. So, too, will outreach on digital media tools such as Facebook, Instagram, and Twitter. Flooding the market with your good works will help not only to burnish your overall image; it will also cause the news you want aired to show up higher in search engine rankings.

We'll now turn to a series of profiles in which a company's reputation was threatened. The intent is, as Eleanor Roosevelt put it, "Learn from the mistakes of others. You can't live long enough to make them all yourself."

Risky Business

What happens when hackers successfully gain access to confidential consumer information entrusted to your company? The health insurer Anthem learned the hard way over the course of several weeks in December 2014 when confronted with a cyberattack on its customer records. The database in question held records for as many as 80 million current and former policyholders.

The hack attack brought reminders of a similar problem encountered by Anthem in 2013. In that instance, the company was fined $1.7 million by federal officials for allowing unauthorized workers access to confidential records.

According to a website developed for the company, "The information accessed may have included names, dates of birth, Social Security numbers, health care ID numbers, home addresses, email addresses, employment information, including income data. We have no reason to believe credit card or banking information was compromised, nor is there evidence at this time that medical information such as claims, test results, or diagnostic codes, was targeted or obtained."

Anthem acknowledged that its database was not encrypted. This drew fire from cybersecurity experts who view this as Data Security 101, especially when sensitive records such as medical information are involved.

Anthem had little capital in its goodwill bank, given the previous breach and its reputation for less than stellar customer service.

What steps could the company have taken to mitigate reputational damage? First, it needed to be prepared to communicate fully and openly with customers affected by the hack. News accounts indicated that some Anthem customers received email notification relatively soon after the discovery. Not all did, however (as this author – an Anthem policyholder – can attest).

Next, the C-suite should have insisted on plotting a communications strategy in advance, setting forth what they were capable of doing internally and what plans they had for getting external help in areas like message development. Of course, they also needed to decide what to say before they said it.

A CEO's Risky Behavior

Your CEO is caught having an affair. Talk about a risky proposition (double entendre intended). His peccadilloes stomped all over your planned new product launch. So much for its smooth addition to your revenue stream.

Rumors had been circulating for some time that your supposedly happily married CEO strayed. His torrid extramarital affair with his long-time executive assistant was confirmed when a corporate responsibility gadfly tweeted video of a romantic tête-à-tête between the two lovebirds. The tweet quickly went viral. Did your tormentor time its release to coincide with your product launch? It's possible, though it really doesn't matter now, for the damage has been done.

On a personal financial level, how much do you think this dilemma will affect your leader's next performance and salary review by your board? He could be in line to lose out on some serious cash.

Your primary trade association cancelled the CEO's scheduled keynote speech to its annual meeting, diplomatically citing "last minute scheduling conflicts." At least they didn't refer to him as the laughingstock of your industry, as others have.

An interview on CNBC, which took your communications staff weeks to cultivate, is dead. It's not that CNBC doesn't want an interview; they certainly do. Their current interest, however, rests not with your new product launch, but with your chief's personal travails. You cancel his appearance.

Meanwhile, the gadfly who circulated the video – long a thorn in your company's side – is riding high on the media circuit discussing his triumph. Thanks to your CEO's recklessness, your tormentor now has a bigger platform than ever to spread his antagonistic thoughts.

What to do? Your CEO has to face the music for this in flagrante indiscretion. If he is adept at parrying tough questions, schedule an interview with a relatively friendly trade publication. If he is easily tongue-tied, issue a statement.

It's also a good idea to seek out one of the CEO's respected peers, and suggest a series of heart-to-heart talks. Contemporaries can often persuade proper actions where others fail.

Turning attention back to rumors, it is instructive to note Charles Fombrun's formulation of how they spread. He writes that rumors propagate in three stages. First is simplification where the story shrinks and details become fuzzy. Second comes exaggeration in which details regain their edge and become more dramatic. The third phase is interpretation which creates stereotypes that support the rumor monger's point of view. Bear this construct in mind the next time you hear rumors reported in the media. It is uncanny how often cries of "fake news" follow this rumor mongering pattern.

Devoting more budget resources toward communications during a crisis is also a must. Other executives will need to step forward as the public voice of your firm for now. This means more work for your communications shop as they (and the external communications consultants you use) need to rapidly improve the communications skills of your C-suite lineup.

So You Want to Be an Influencer

One good way to inoculate your business against reputational risk is to persuade your C-suite executives to raise their thought leadership profiles.

The financial benefits of this endeavor can be difficult to quantify. It makes sense that your company will gain sales if your leadership is front and center in the public's consciousness (assuming that image is positive, of course).

And they will no doubt increase their own marketability (and, therefore, income) whether at your company or at their next landing spot when viewed as a top thinker.

You have my permission to smile broadly when the boss tells you she wants a more upbeat public image. There's nothing wrong with that since reputational benefits are likely to accrue to both her and the company.

Here's where things get tricky. She expects the communications staff to deliver on that impulse, which means your reputation hangs in the balance, too. If the effort succeeds, you have punched a golden career ticket, living for decades off the ability to say you worked for the now-great woman. If things go south, however, you can bet that your communications officers will be relocated to what amounts to a corporate Siberia.

There are three basic means of raising one's thought leadership profile. The first is speaking. So set up the leadership with speeches to key audiences in formats that show them at their best. The second technique is writing. While their names appear in the byline, in many cases your communications shop will do most of the writing. Here again, target your audiences with care. The third approach involves research. Agreed, this isn't for everyone. Yet if your CEO has a pet issue and the least inclination to dig deep into it, get your research team to work and foster that drive. Then publish the findings under her banner in an appropriate journal and send her out on the hustings to talk about it.

The Renegade Worker Strikes

This is really a reputational pickle. One of your workers has tweeted about drunken escapades at your employee development retreat.

A series of ribald Twitter messages over a one-hour period exposed (pardon the pun) a hearty evening of drinking games, slurs about management, and libertine liaisons. All this occurred during your annual offsite employee development session.

Externally, your top customers have pledged to review their business relationship with you. In fact, one has already pulled out of negotiations for a big contract scheduled to commence next year.

Plus, all that budget dedicated to the employee retreat is down the drain. Who can take things seriously with everyone glued to their phones and the bawdy photo display? The tech-savvy offender took advantage of

Twitter's video capability to shoot several clips that laid bare (oops, please pardon again) the fun and games for the whole world to see.

There goes your company's heretofore squeaky clean image. Your CEO, who, of course, had no idea this was happening, has vowed that heads will roll. Those heads include not only the offending tweet meister and his co-stars in the video, but the team that organized the retreat; they were held responsible for trying to create a "fun" experience that served to encourage the tawdry behavior.

Naturally, the tweets – especially the videos – went viral. The most common refrain came from those who, tongue-in-cheek, wondered how they could get a job at such a laid back workplace.

It's time to face the music. Your C-suite team has to explain how this happened and to ensure shaky customers how it will work to prevent future occurrences. It's time to activate your crisis communications plan. Part of this plan should involve a rapid response via digital media channels. In this instance, using Twitter to apologize to your customers and explain how you plan to prevent similar exploits in the future is mandatory.

A Shooter on the Loose

A hospitalized prisoner escapes from Inova Fairfax Hospital, wrestles away a guard's gun, fires a shot, and flees. Neighbors of the suburban Washington, D.C., hospital were on high alert. And for good reason as the escapee carjacked a local woman.

A massive police presence followed the getaway, with wall-to-wall coverage on local TV news stations. The jailbird was captured hours later on a bus in a Washington neighborhood. Fortunately, no one else was harmed.

All access was restricted into and out of the hospital until matters clarified. In addition, police with military-style gear combed the surrounding area, giving the TV camera crews great opportunities for vivid footage.

In the end, Inova Fairfax experienced very little negative reaction. One big reason: As reported by the *Washington Business Journal*, hospital executives had just conducted a review of its crisis communications efforts the previous day.

What lessons can you take away from studying this well-handled crisis? First, follow the playbook reportedly used by Inova Fairfax. While a shooter on the loose is bound to engender some degree of alarm, hospital executives minimized any panic thanks to advance preparations. Such actions as contacting the police and securing the facility became instant reactions, not wild guesses.

In addition, confusion was minimized since the organization's executive team knew in advance that it would need to take steps such as postponing non-emergency surgery in the event of a crisis at the facility. A hospital security official told the *Washington Business Journal*, "(P)art of the plan is securing the patient, closing doors and whatnot, so if there's a perpetrator running through the building, we don't want there to be opportunities. We let the patients know what's going on. If we need to, we turn out lights, etc. We have an operational plan to do that. And it worked extremely well."

Assessing feedback once conditions have eased is imperative. Following any crisis, put your plan through the wringer to weigh how it worked. As CEO Patrick Christiansen put it, "That plan should be continuously reviewed, not something that's just put on the shelf."

Headline Risk

In 2014, flawed ignition switches led General Motors to recall over 2.5 million vehicles. Company CEO Mary Barra was roasted by Congressional committees interested in the company's woes, and the company was pounded by weeks of negative headlines.

To encourage GM owners to replace the faulty switches, the manufacturer offered $25 gift certificates for various retailers. My trusty calculator tells me that figure times 2.5 million vehicles comes to a cool $62.5 million. That may not break the bank at an outfit like GM. All the same, it's hardly chump change.

It is often difficult to quantify the dollar damage caused by episodes such as the GM recall. Not this time. Early in 2014, *Barron's* guessed that General Motors stock could gain 30 percent in value. So much for that crystal ball. In reality, the stock price dipped from its January 2014 level of $40.03 to a year-end value of $34.84.

The investor relations community calls this "headline risk," meaning the danger of damage from a series of negative news reports. That industry uses that term of art to describe one manifestation of reputational risk.

This is a case in which some people had to walk the plank. CEO Barra canned 15 top GM executives and reprimanded five others due to this snafu. If you're in the C-suite and you deem such moves necessary, make sure to alert your communications staff since they are the ones charged with dealing with the fallout.

Rarely can a Congressional hearing be equated with a genteel afternoon tea. When the pleasure of your presence is requested by a Congressional committee, pull out all the stops when preparing. See Chapter Five on advocacy for a deeper dive.

In Mary Barra, GM had the advantage of a CEO capable of exhibiting a caring attitude. She was featured in a series of short videos targeted toward GM car owners that took advantage of her ability to speak on a human level. When your crisis strikes, consider both the communicators and the communications channels you have at your disposal, and decide which ones to lean on.

A Toxic Stew of Events

One of the classic reputational risks involves a toxic chemical spill polluting local streams. Your company is in the crosshairs when it's traced to your manufacturing plant. You're certainly staring at high costs for a massive cleanup as well as hefty fines from federal, state, and local regulators.

Talk about business disruption. The plant is shut down indefinitely. Additionally, the markets lose faith in your ability to tend to your core business. The stock price tumbles, your quarterly financial report is pummeled by the fines and cleanup outlays, and employee bonuses are a thing of the past.

No one in the local community trusts you any longer. The environmental activists who had been warning for years that your plant was an accident waiting to happen are crowing, having been proven right. Remember those transition plans you were working on when your CEO made it known he wanted to retire next year? How many high quality CEO candidates will want to jump on board this sinking ship?

Your future also includes tighter regulatory scrutiny from every government body imaginable. Your external communications channels will be monitored closely. As a matter of fact, the next misstep could spell doom for the business.

Short of pulling your hair and rending your garments, what can you do? This crisis falls into the category of eminently predictable, so pull out your crisis plan immediately and follow it. What's that you say? You haven't prepared for how you'll communicate with your workers, community, and regulators? Well, that's a problem.

Decide who has responsibility for talking with the press and public. Put them front and center, and instruct everyone else to hold their fire and refer all questions to your public faces.

Remember to hold that series of media training workshops before any risk becomes evident. One sure way to damage your reputation permanently: Wait until problems arise before grooming your spokespeople.

Can We Talk Off the Record?

We cover the use of "off the record" when dealing with reporters more fully in Chapter Three. Here's an example where it backfired when used by an incapable, too-smart-by-half executive.

An official for the car service Uber ostensibly thought he was off the record when speaking to a group of reporters in November 2014. Not so.

Uber, a company with a reputation for sharp elbows, dug itself a deep hole when senior vice president Emil Michael floated the idea that the firm secretly hire opposition researchers to investigate the private lives of journalists critical of the company.

Michael claimed that his remarks were off the record. *BuzzFeed*, however, stated that it had agreed to no such conditions and that it was free to publish his comments. Important reminder: Any agreement to go off the record must be hashed out before an interview begins, and both parties must positively affirm those ground rules.

Ironically, the comments came at a time when Uber was trying to soften its image in the press. Threatening to dig up dirt on reporters is hardly a means to that end. The ham-handed effort served to heighten suspicion, not reduce it.

This image was further hindered when Michael issued a statement reacting to the revelations. According to *Vanity Fair*, he cited "sensationalistic media coverage" and argued that the comments "do not reflect my actual views and have no relation to the company's views or approach." He also said, "They were wrong no matter the circumstance and I regret them."

Further, Michael hardly endeared his company to the military, where he served on an advisory body known as the Defense Business Board. As then-Pentagon spokesman John Kirby said in a *BuzzFeed* article, "We do not associate ourselves with the comments Mr. Michael made or the views they represent."

Instances like this sometimes happen when executives are too smart for their own good (or think they are too smart). You must impress upon your C-suite the rules of the media relations road.

Never, ever allow anyone but your communications professionals to negotiate these rules. It doesn't matter how big a genius your executives think they may be. The simple fact is they are not qualified to negotiate in this realm.

Be prepared should comments go public. Off the record can be a useful tool for steering a reporter in a certain direction. But inform your leadership that they are never to say something they would regret reading in a reporter's Twitter feed or on the front page.

Scoring in the Opponent's Goal

FIFA, soccer's worldwide governing body, was hit with a red card for a corruption scandal in May 2015. The organization's alleged culture of corruption was perhaps the worst-kept secret in the sporting world. Then U.S. and Swiss officials dropped the hammer.

Sponsors including Adidas, Anheuser-Busch, Coca-Cola, Hyundai, and Visa all pledged to take fresh looks at their multi-million dollar deals. Follow through on their part would be highly damaging to FIFA. However, follow through absent any additional outside pressure was questionable. Companies as savvy as these sponsors could hardly be shocked to learn of the shady dealings that had been so well publicized over a period of years.

Organizations sometimes find themselves trapped by the wrong leaders in place at the wrong time. Case in point: former FIFA President Joseph "Sepp" Blatter, who tried to run away from the mess faster than Usain Bolt. "We, or I, cannot monitor everyone all of the time. If people want to do wrong, they will also try to hide it," said Blatter.

There is more than external damage in play here. Internally, the U.S. Soccer Federation threw its support to Blatter's opponent during FIFA elections. It was to no immediate avail, as Blatter was elected to a fifth term, though he did an abrupt about-face and resigned. Still, future relations are likely to be rocky, serving to further weaken FIFA's reputation and effectiveness.

When you see wrongdoing in your company, sound the alarm. In some instances, particularly in regulated industries or where you have a fiduciary responsibility, you may have a legal obligation to do so.

As a senior communications or public affairs official in your firm, it is your responsibility to speak truth to power. Your C-suite may not want to hear bad news or confront sticky situations. It's up to you to make them listen. If you need some support, bring in a communications consultant who is unafraid to have those conversations.

How Much Risk Is Your Business Willing to Assume?

Your communications strategy and your message must be airtight when advocating in the court of public opinion. It's risky business. Your reputation, your business goals – your very career – are at stake.

Some internal communications teams are up to the job; some are not, due to anything from inexperience to incompetence to indifference. That's why many larger businesses rely on consultants experienced in communications strategy. It's what smart businesses do.

When you decide to seek outside counsel, be alert to a couple of factors. Make sure your consultant will not slough off your program to junior account team staffers, and that he will not risk your reputation with a group of nebulous "associates" you'll never meet. Insist on working with an experienced principal you know and can trust.

Your consultant should work with you to determine what reputational strengths you already possess, and which areas you need to sharpen. Ensure that your agreement outlines a strategic program suited to your specific needs while maintaining a degree of flexibility for the inevitable mid-course corrections. My belief is that, as the consultant, I should do the heavy lifting when it comes to strategy, freeing you to implement your plans.

Calling on outside consultants for help with communications strategy makes sense if your company confronts the following hurdles:

- The CEO who is not satisfied with his company's message development and delivery.
- The C-suite leader trying to get her communications and public affairs teams on the same page.
- The business that needs an unbiased point of view on where your communications risks and rewards lurk.
- The corporate leader frustrated with getting his legal, finance, or marketing team to deliver a concise, consistent message.
- The firm concerned with ramping up its professional development choices.
- A technical expert who shies away from media interviews.
- C-suite executives with high stakes speaking or media opportunities staring them in the face.
- Businesses that confront challenges onboarding communications and government relations staffers.
- Communications teams that tremble when trying to counsel the C-suite.
- The government relations executive who needs to ramp up the performance of her advocates when they deal with policymakers.

Your path toward improvement may mean working with your consultant once a week, once a month, or anything in between. You may even decide to bring him on site for a week or two initially. He should also be readily accessible by telephone, video conference, and email.

Secure Your Reputational Insurance Coverage Now – Before You Need It

Once upon a time, I worked in the field of insurance regulation, so I know how important it is to get insurance coverage right.

Your business has insurance for fire, cyberattacks, worker injury, and a laundry list of other eventualities. But are you insured in the event of a communications crisis that threatens your treasured reputation?

Who is the "insurance carrier" capable of taking care of you when someone in your company commits a communications faux pas? More important, who can you turn to for sage advice on how to prepare for the inevitable catastrophe? You don't know when it will take place or exactly what form it will take. But admit it, you know it's coming. In the colorful phrasing of former President Lyndon Johnson, "I once told Nixon that the presidency is like being a jackass caught in a hail storm. You've got to just stand there and take it."

Here are just a few examples of reputational dings you should strive to prevent, or at least minimize:

- Ill-advised quotes from your spokespeople in the newspaper.
- Failure to achieve your public policy objectives.
- A tarnished reputation and stalled career for your CEO.
- Loss of your company's leadership position in your industry.
- High employee turnover due to lack of professional development opportunities.

You get the picture. And it's not a pretty one for those who stubbornly refuse to solidify their reputation.

What's the solution? Pay attention to your reputational risks before you need to. On a personal level, if your house is in a flood plain and you don't take out flood insurance, it's too late. When that once-in-a-hundred-year monsoon strikes, you're wiped out. Your house, your cars, your personal belongings – gone. Those who have the foresight to purchase flood insurance are in much better shape. Life won't be easy, but it will be manageable.

So it goes with communicating to preserve your reputation. Line up your insurance coverage preemptively. That crisis, whatever it may be, will be easier to deal with when you do. You need a plan that sets forth how to act when crisis strikes, and how to gauge your risk and plan for it in advance. Don't leave it at that. You check your insurance coverage at least once a year. So should you have regular examinations of your communications "insurance policy."

A May 9, 2018, *Nonprofit Quarterly* article ("Risk Leadership: A Necessary Embrace for Nonprofit Leaders") cites the views of Michele Braun, director of Manhattanville College's Institute for Managing Risk. The piece focuses on non-profit leaders, though remains instructive for C-suite business executives, too. It suggests a few key questions the C-suite should ask of their companies. They include anticipating risks that could cripple the business, risks that can help achieve overall goals, how risk is assessed and dealt with, and a commitment to stay alert to potential risks.

Braun recommends a yearly examination of hazards you might face. This exam encompasses conversations among all staff from the CEO on down, a review of new opportunities and challenges, and the need to call upon external experts for their unique perspectives.

The article points out that, while risk is almost universally viewed as a negative factor, it also presents opportunities for growth. I suggest these opportunities could include growth of the business, inauguration of a new product or service, advocacy of legislation that makes it over the finish line, and – of prime importance – a healthier corporate reputation.

Now's the time to make your move and ensure your reputation. You never know when that flood is going to strike.

Your Move

My hope is that this chapter will serve as a springboard for civil, reasoned, intelligent (and yes, sometimes impassioned) discussion about the reputational risks businesses face. Read, ponder, synthesize, and discuss. Then (and here's the important part), act!

What specific steps can you take?

- Use these thoughts as a guide to help your company and its people chart your course.
- Share this research with colleagues, both external and internal.
- Suggest this as a program topic at a professional society to which you belong.
- Initiate open discussions with your C-suite, especially if you currently lack a reputational risk plan.

Five for the Future

As you discovered in Chapter Nine, every business encounters risk. The challenge is to minimize and mitigate it as much as possible. Use these "Five for the Future" discussion questions to help you sustain your C-suite's professional development over the long run. Discuss these issues with co-workers, professional colleagues, mentors, and in your own mind:

1. What are the most obvious risks your business faces?
2. Dig deeper and think about some of the risks that are not so obvious. What can you do to prepare for them?
3. What types of scenarios can you play out to help reduce your risk?

4.   What is the risk profile of your C-suite? Are your leaders risk takers or do they tend to be risk averse?

5.   How often should you formally examine your risk profile?

Bonus content

Risk is everywhere. Sometimes it's easy to tune out the alarm bells. You'll discover some extra pointers to help you tune in at www.barkscomm.com/APlusBonus for your copy of "Your Communications Strategy: 10 Warning Signs."

CHAPTER 10

CRISIS COMMUNICATION

Several years ago, my wife worked in the planning department for a small town government. One of the local characters about town was a fellow nicknamed Cowboy. He'd roam the streets all day long, hobnobbing with anyone and everyone. The locals knew that making eye contact risked a lengthy, one-way conversation.

Yet, pesky though he could be, Cowboy served a valuable municipal function. He acted like an early warning system. His traipsing around town gave him the lowdown when crises large and small arose – anything from flooding in the creek that ran through town to a broken parking meter.

To this day, my wife and her former colleagues recall Cowboy routinely bursting into the town office, issuing his trademark, "I got some bad news for you guys!"

Who's your Cowboy? Who in your company makes the rounds and is in position to sound an early alarm bell? In large firms it may be the recent college grad who delivers the mail. Perhaps it's the executive assistant who knows and sees all. In one of my former workplaces, it was one of the senior lawyers who had an innate knack for getting the scoop. The point is you need a system for keeping your finger on the pulse of your business lest you get blindsided by your next crisis.

As you know by now, this volume is not intended as a textbook. Nonetheless, a definition for "crisis" is useful to ensure author and reader are on the same page (pardon the pun). Following are some of the traits used to classify a crisis.

It must have a quick onset, and be unforeseen and unwanted. It calls for quick decisions. While the odds of the event occurring are low, its impact is extremely high. A crisis throws a wrench into your day-to-day patterns. It diverts you from working toward your highest priorities. It threatens your company's profits, prosperity, and very survival. If you ignore the situation, things will continue to worsen. It induces stress throughout your business, from the C-suite to the IT department to the reception desk.

And there's no escaping it. News of a crisis spreads more rapidly than in the past due to factors like cell phone video, Twitter hashtags, and blogs covering any issue imaginable.

On the other hand, there may be times when your leadership senses a crisis that is merely an irritant. Your job as the resident communications expert is to talk them down off the ledge and keep a sense of perspective. You run the risk of making things worse by spotlighting it or overreacting. Remember, your external audiences know far less about the details of your situation than you do.

A 2018 Deloitte Global survey found, citing *The Wall Street Journal* from June 21, 2018, "While 90% of the respondents expressed confidence in their organization's ability to address major trouble, the survey of 523 senior executives involved in risk, crisis management and business continuity found just 17% said their organization tested its crisis planning."

Expect rumors, some of them unfounded, to abound. How can you try to correct such misperceptions? Here are some options at your disposal, courtesy of *Crisis Communications: A Casebook Approach* by Kathleen Fearn-Banks. You obviously need to determine which steps make the most sense in your specific instance:

- Broadcast information that is as thorough and accurate as possible.
- Assess the situation. Determine how and where it began, and who is involved.
- Gauge the level of threat to your business. Could this be its death knell?
- Ignore the rumors. Sometimes they go away on their own. A denial could serve to magnify the issue.
- Refute the rumor in no uncertain terms. Make sure you can prove your point.
- Persuade a third party – perhaps an academic or former government official – to discredit the gossip.

Conducting a crisis pre-mortem is a good idea. This is a blue sky exercise that asks your C-suite to imagine a time one year from now. A crisis has taken place and your plan failed miserably. Have them take 15 minutes to write down (yes, everyone writes before discussion takes place) why the plan flopped, and instruct them to be specific.

Make This Crisis Disappear

Whether they rely on employees or consultants, some C-suite executives labor under the impression that communications experts can snap their fingers and make a crisis go away. "Good night and good luck," in the words of CBS News legend Edward R. Murrow.

While it's nice to feel such confidence in our abilities, neither I nor any of my colleagues have a magic wand capable of such illusion. Oh, we may be able to help minimize its impact, depending on the precise situation, by hammering out a clear message and offering guidance on how to deliver it. But sending it into oblivion? Not going to happen.

Calamity is on its way, make no mistake. You can never know exactly where or when, but it's around the corner. A random one-week sampling of articles in *The Washington Post* in July 2018 unearthed more than 120 mentions of "crisis" covering issues from politics, medicine, sports, education, and plenty more. Crises are everywhere in the news. Might yours be next?

Getting Your CEO to See the Light

This uncertainty can prove especially vexing for internal staff who, in many cases, don't have the heft to sit the boss down and speak the unvarnished truth. After all, they probably like having a job, and challenging the big kahuna can place one's immediate employment prospects on shaky ground.

The fact remains that sometimes our job involves managing expectations and getting executives to see the real-world picture.

The midst of a crisis is not the time for detailed planning efforts, which means that you need to prepare and rehearse your crisis communications plan in advance. What are some methods for opening your boss' eyes that you can arrange ahead of time?

Bring evidence to bear from similar crises. Keep a file on happenings in the news that touch on situations you might anticipate. When your calamity strikes, quickly pull out the clips that most closely parallel your current plight.

Actively involve your top brass in your crisis messaging efforts. Teach them that your message will evolve rapidly as new developments come to light. Be ready for some long hours and intense discussions. Depending on the severity of the situation, this is one instance where you need to bring in the lawyers for messaging purposes since legal issues may well be involved. However, don't give your legal eagles veto power over your message. Their job is to keep you out of trouble from the law. They are not necessarily experts in arguing in the court of public opinion. That's your job as the resident communications expert.

Securing Your CEO's Confidence

Find one of your CEO's peers who can talk sense into them. It's a good idea to keep these helpers on your speed dial. Develop relationships with their communications staffers so that both of you can encourage occasional conversations about communications successes and challenges. When crisis hits, use that leverage.

Prepare your spokespeople. Yes, you should run them through an emergency media training refresher at the onset of your crisis. You should also insist that all your spokespeople routinely participate in a sustained training program. If you wait until the crisis manifests, you lose.

Get your executives' insights into likely allies and adversaries. The more public support you can muster and the better you can anticipate where attacks will originate, the higher the likelihood of navigating your crisis with fewer negative consequences.

Finally, hire a consultant with broader view who can speak truth to your executives. Experienced consultants won't shy away from working through the tough issues.

Some executives believe that a crisis demands an apology. Others would never dream of saying they are remorseful for anything. Similarly, some communications consultants swear that apology is necessary in every instance. This is largely the old school approach where everything fit neatly into a trite crisis response format. Other communicators argue that an apology needs to be considered on a case-by-case basis. Indeed, online sniping about this "to apologize or not to apologize" difference of opinion is easy to unearth. I come down on the side of the latter camp since every situation is different and demands a unique response.

Your company is not likely to emerge from a crisis unscathed. Your reputation and your revenues may take a hit, and you need to make the head-in-the-sand boss understand that. Sound crisis management works to lessen the shock. But making it go away? Sorry, that's a fool's dream.

Anticipating the Severity of Your Crisis

When a crisis mushrooms, there is a bounty of questions you need to consider, and consider fast. Every crisis is different, so some of these questions may not apply in your case. Of course, you may have other issues that are unique to you:

- How can you begin to prepare ahead of time?

- Have you suffered any physical or infrastructure harm?
- Is there a product recall involved?
- Can your existing resources, both financial and human, handle the crush or do you need to bring in outside help or boost your budget?

Always assume that the press will somehow learn of your dilemma even if it's not something spectacularly evident like a plant explosion or a mass shooting. There are many and complex issues when trying to sate the scribe tribe. Among them:

- Is media interest confined to your local press or is this story going national or global?
- What will the regional and local press want from you? And what angle is the national press taking?
- How soon will they catch on to your plight?
- What do you say if you need to respond instantly? Do you have a holding statement at hand?
- Are your spokespeople equipped to handle questions from the press?
- Do you have a media strategy consultant on speed dial to help you manage the media crush, and to game out potential scenarios in advance?
- What will happen if you try to stonewall reporters?
- Which of your spokespeople should deliver bad news?
- If death or injury has occurred, how will your company comfort relatives?
- Should photographers have access to the scene of any catastrophe?
- When the media starts to blame you, how do you react?
- The governor or president wants to visit the scene of the carnage. How do you handle that?
- An organization with which you always disagree launches a media campaign against you. Should you respond? If so, how?
- Taking the long view, what do you think the story will look like weeks, months, or years down the road?
- Once the crisis has abated, how can you use it to help ease you through future disasters?

You also need to decide whether the situation requires quick response, deferred response, or no response on your part. Also consider whether any actions you take should be short- or long-term, and whether any public pronouncements are indicated and, if so, how immediate they have to be.

Helping Your Board Weather a Media Storm

Financial malfeasance is discovered at your company. One of your board members is slapped with a sexual harassment lawsuit. A staff member has unintentionally leaked news that places your business in a bad light. A seemingly small consumer complaint has suddenly gone viral on YouTube. A natural disaster has knocked out your manufacturing capability.

What do many firms do when confronted with such crises? They duck. Or they reach for the baling wire and chewing gum. As you may surmise, these approaches rarely work.

It may be impossible to know when a crisis will occur or just what it might be: An IT failure, a lawsuit, a fire at your warehouse that claims lives, an executive misstep, a scuffle with a renegade shareholder, a terrorist attack, pickets outside your plant gates, a sudden interest on the part of Congressional overseers, a political tempest. Whatever the dilemma, don't let yourself fall into the trap of hiding your head in the sand. It's coming. And the health of your business, your industry, and your career may well hang in the balance.

You will hear some say that a crisis is an opportunity. Nonsense. A crisis is a crisis. It is not easy to battle through it, but battle you must for the sake of your company's future.

Crises: A Question of When, Not Whether

All organizations face crises, from small to large, for catastrophes come in all shapes and sizes. What may be only a minor irritation for a Fortune 500 corporation could decimate a smaller firm. An example: A mid-level manager at a well-known corporation is charged with discrimination, doling out favorable assignments to younger staffers while forcing older employees to do drudgery work, with the intent of pushing them out the door. While this may have an impact on that department, a larger group can absorb much of the blowback, with the event never reaching the headlines.

Consider, however, this same scenario in a smaller business where the CEO is charged with the same offense, and is forced to resign. What will the company say publicly about that resignation? Don't you think the trade press covering the industry will have a few questions? And might the Twitter stream for that sector light up with rumors?

The point here is you must try to get a grip on what constitutes a crisis for you. Sure, a CFO charged with embezzlement, a colleague slapped with a sexual harassment suit based on conduct at your employee retreat, and a toxic emission at one of your facilities all qualify. But so, too, might such seemingly smaller occurrences as the incapacity of a key board member or illegal drug use in the long ago past by one of your vice presidents. Such revelations have derailed many once-promising careers, including that of a potential Supreme Court justice.

In her *Crisis Communications: A Casebook Approach*, Fearn-Banks describes three potential outcomes of a crisis:

1. Your company goes out of business, and your CEO is subjected to a perp walk.
2. The company survives but limps along with a damaged reputation (for both the firm and the workers) as well as a lessened financial capacity.
3. You fight the good fight and restore your reputation in the court of public opinion.

Your reputation – personally and organizationally – is at stake. For some businesses, the crisis is but the first step in a cascading series of events that make matters even worse. It causes shareholders to lose faith, sends your valuation into the toilet, and spirals ever downward. Or it can lead partners to shun you, shutting you out of speaking at industry conferences and taking away your position as chair of that key committee within your trade association.

The Perils of an Unprepared Board

What could worsen a crisis? Ask yourself this question: To what extent do your board members and executive staff have knowledge of how to deal with reporters, particularly when things turn calamitous? Encourage them to think like newsman Ed Bradley: "I will not go into a story unprepared. I will do my homework, and that's something I learned at an early age."

Be honest with yourself here. If you have not engaged in strategic media training for your board members, key committee chairs, C-suite, and other key spokespeople, you are placing your company's reputation in jeopardy. If your communications staff is experienced and savvy enough, you may opt to conduct such sessions internally. Otherwise, it is well worth it to engage on a regular basis a consultant dedicated solely to the craft of strategic communications training.

Regardless of your political leanings, the job done under pressure by New Jersey Gov. Chris Christie in the aftermath of Hurricane Sandy serves as a model for proper crisis management. Tell your public what you know and what you don't know. Provide frequent updates with breaking developments. Tell the public what they should do.

In the case of Hurricane Sandy, the public involved was the citizenry of New Jersey. In your case, it may be your customers, a geographical area impacted by the crisis (in the case of a plant closure, for instance), or public officials who need to be reassured that you are on top of matters.

What is a company to do to get its key spokespeople up to speed in preparation for a crisis? First, acknowledge that you will not know all the facts. Early reports may be spotty or even erroneous, so you must perform your due diligence when it comes to fact checking. Always be honest even when events place you in a less than favorable light. And avoid hypotheticals. If you don't have confirmed facts, tell the media that you will offer updates as events warrant.

Show some empathy to show that you care about those affected. This assumes that you actually do care. Some organizations don't. If you're in that category, good luck to you.

Next, ensure that your communications and public affairs departments collaborate with your lawyers. Typically, the lawyers advise that you say nothing, though there are exceptions when the roles are reversed. Be prepared to lose in the court of public opinion if you follow the wrong path.

Some crisis consultants advise having a sole mouthpiece as your company's face to the public. I disagree. To be sure, you need to speak with a single voice, which mandates a clear and consistent message. But, unless your crisis is small and relatively contained, it's just too much pressure and too much of an energy-sapping chore for a single individual to be available around the clock and in every locale.

Work diligently to make your message part of the story the media tells. Sticking your head in the sand is for losers since it allows the media to quote your adversaries unfettered. Use digital media channels to push out updates. Sources such as Facebook, Instagram, LinkedIn groups, and Twitter can help.

In the first phase of a disaster, you'll need a holding statement. This is essentially boilerplate language used to give you something to say without putting your foot in your mouth. It reads along the lines of: "We are working to get this incident under control and to gather the facts. The safety of our community, our customers, our neighbors, and our workers comes first. We will get back to you at [a time certain] with an update."

As information flows in, tell your public where you plan to go from here. Go beyond a "just the facts, ma'am" approach. Paint a vision showing how you aim to get out from under the crisis and evade future problems.

Never Put Off Until Tomorrow ...

Gather the resources you need now, before the storm strikes. Residents of the Midwest know how to prepare for tornadoes ahead of time. They build storm cellars and know what to do when heavy weather threatens and the storm sirens blare. Waiting until the tornado is overhead to build that storm cellar is not an option. In the words of Emerson, "We learn geology after the earthquake."

Steel yourself for your next storm by beginning work on your crisis communications plan today. If you already have one, congratulations. If you haven't updated it recently, you have some work to do.

While you won't be able to anticipate the precise catastrophe or exactly when it will strike, you will put yourself in position to emerge with as little tarnish as possible if you plan and prepare your board members and other spokespeople in advance.

Decide now which board members, executives, and communications staff need to be intimately involved in both planning and execution, and which communications consultants you will engage to help you manage the tough times.

One guarantee: A crisis is on the way. Will your company come out the other side in good shape?

Communicating During a Hack Attack

One particularly insidious crisis is the cyberattack. It's not like the impact from an industrial accident or a hurricane. When your business is hit online, you may not learn about it for months. And that's if your tech team is on the ball.

Every business has already battled or will soon face a cybercrisis, so let's use this model as an example of how to act when the stuff hits the fan.

Cybercrime is now a big business. Life was easier when it was just un-shaven, smelly guys subsisting on Cheetos and Peanut M&M's living in their parents' basements. These days you're in for a business-to-business brawl or, even more dangerous, a sophisticated attack launched by a foreign government.

Today's executives dread cybercrime, with many viewing it as the number one threat to the business. The odds are strong that you are going to be affected at some point, by either an external or internal hack.

You have a plethora of resources at your disposal that cover certain aspects of batting back a hack attack – insurance that covers some of the damages, guidance from federal authorities as to your legal reporting re-quirements, and an ever-growing population of companies eager to (alleged-ly) protect you.

The hard truth is, however, few if any of those resources are capable of walking you through the fallout of what it takes to communicate when hackers worm their way into your systems. Let us examine that essential yet oft-ignored aspect – managing the communications component of the crisis, for how you communicate with your stakeholders in the near- and long-term could spell the difference between survival and chronic struggle.

When, Not If

Your business is going to experience a cyberattack. It may occur today, tomorrow, or several months from now. Are you a doubter? Try these examples on for size:

- A health insurer that loses track of confidential policyholder data.
- A retail outlet that suffers theft of customer credit card records.
- An online small business that is forced to devote massive resources and months to overcoming a nefarious hacker.
- A medical device manufacturer whose products – and more importantly, patient safety – are compromised.
- The internal threat, in which one of your workers sells access to your data for a few thousand dollars.
- Another internal threat where the hacker gives one of your workers a thumb drive (and a bounty) to inject malware into your system.
- A problem your chief risk officer never saw coming.
- You discover you've been victimized by ransomware, a situation in which black hats put a "time bomb" in your system that activates after your backups are too old to do any good. Do you want the solution? Pay the blackmail to the not-so-nice man.

Are you still a doubter? Don't take my word for it. Ask executives at Anthem, Equifax, Medtronic, Target, Yahoo, and a plethora of other firms. The above examples are not fantasy. Those businesses and the marketplaces that rely on them paid the price of a hack attack. They suffered these all too real impacts:

- Shrinking revenues.
- Lost customers.
- Untold financial pain.
- Psychic anguish.
- Time and productivity costs.
- A tarnished reputation, both for your firm and for your executives' career arcs.

A 21st Century Gold Rush

Why do you think insurers now offer cyber risk seminars that offer insight into potential cyber threats, how to combat them, and their regulatory ramifications? Yes, there's gold in them thar cyberhills.

What's on the cybersecurity horizon? Things are not getting any easier as hackers become more sophisticated and pursue targets that have yet to harden themselves.

Your business plan likely sets forth the information technology (IT) resources you'll rely on when hackers hit. Some businesses stop there. Big mistake.

Your discovery of and recovery from the attack may be altogether elegant. Your technical team may succeed in fending off or minimizing negative consequences. Regardless, you're going to come under fire from customers, shareholders, industry analysts ... perhaps even government regulators.

Yes, you may lose intellectual property, suffer theft of credit card information, and become subject to a slew of governmental oversight hearings. Of equal import, your good reputation – the one you've taken decades to foster – will be in tatters in a matter of days, if not hours.

Communication Is Key

More and more businesses are developing cybersecurity disaster preparation plans. It's a necessity in this day and age. But if you stop there, you're only fighting part of the battle.

A cyber communications plan is also a must. Just as an overall communications plan guides your business to a better public image, a cyber communications plan spells out how you will react and the steps you will take when hackers assault your systems. Your plan also needs to set forth how likely you deem a particular crisis to be and to evaluate the potential damage it can cause. Fail to devise such a plan and you'll be left scrambling in a panicked and most disorganized manner when catastrophe arises.

Make no mistake, this means a written plan, one that all of your workers can reference. Still, in mid-crisis it is impossible to call up your plan and follow it to the letter. It is a set of guidelines that your staff needs to internalize ahead of time with the understanding that some degree of flexibility will be essential. That is why you need to drill regularly for likely eventualities.

Sadly, relatively little guidance is available about this vital facet of crisis planning. Plug the term "cybersecurity communications plan" into your favorite search engine and you'll see plenty of advice about privacy, securing credit card information, better protecting mobile devices, and fending off email incursions. But you have to scour deep to find anything substantive and helpful about communicating with your publics.

What to Do in the Midst of Your Cybercrisis

The biggest cyber threat cited by many chief information officers is their own staffs. Workers who click on phishing links, visit sketchy websites, or steal data for their own illegal gain scare the bejeebers out of these executives. This, of course, argues that your communications about cybersecurity need to begin before events occur. You must communicate with employees and bring them up to speed on best security practices.

Once the cat is out of the bag, the pace of your communications picks up rapidly. You must be ready with a plan that answers such key questions as:

- How much information can you disclose, both legally and from a business perspective?
- Who is empowered to speak on your business' behalf?
- Who belongs on the team that will craft and continue to refine your message as the crisis unfolds?
- Is there still a way to protect any intellectual property that may have been pilfered?
- What steps can you take to assuage clients and consumers and make them whole if their data has been swiped?

Cyber theft is as much a communications problem as an IT issue. To be sure, you need to include your online security and risk teams as you seek to understand and define your predicament. In most cases, however, these are not the spokespeople you want front and center when explaining things to the world. Jane and John Q. Public don't need a buzzword-laden technical rundown; they need to know how your incident affects them, what you are doing to solve the problem, and what, if anything, they need to do.

Preparation Steps You Need to Heed

Take the long view. This is admittedly a challenge in the day and age of quarterly results and their expectations serving as the benchmark for success or failure. Prudent investments – both in technology and in communications and public affairs capacities – are necessary on a sustained basis.

There is plenty of advice available regarding how to bolster your IT department: Hire more skilled workers, buy that shiny new company's anti-hacker services, tighten your company's email filters.

But there is another crucial question: How can your business fortify its communications strength? There seems to be far less discussion on this matter, so here are some suggestions to help guide you:

- Charge your communications staff with organizing and leading regular simulations surrounding cyber threats. Get firm dates on everyone's calendar well ahead of time, and brook no excuses for absence; attendance is 100 percent mandatory. Depending on the likelihood of the threat, this could mean holding dress rehearsals every quarter, at six-month intervals, or annually.

- Craft your message in anticipation of an attack. While you won't be able to divine the precise nature of your situation, you can and should set a general template that helps you outline what to say when the time comes. Make your message one of the focal points when conducting your simulated drills.

- Decide which executives will be your public face in which situations. It is normally a good idea to place your CEO front and center, unless he is a lost soul as a communicator.

- Hold periodic media training workshops for those executives who will be in the press' line of fire during any cybercrisis. Note that this means more than a "one and done" session. You need ongoing skill sharpening.

- Do your best to assure in advance that your communications, legal, and public affairs teams play nice together. Anticipate disagreements about how much to say when crisis strikes and decide on the proper balance for your state of affairs.

- Nurture relationships throughout your company. Colleagues in other departments can serve as scouts, alerting you to potential problems before they grow or go public. Also, quiz them about scenarios that could befall their departments and work these into your simulations as appropriate.

- Establish a relationship with an experienced communications training consultant who can guide you before, during, and after your cyberattack. If you are under contract with a public affairs or public relations agency, make sure they have someone on staff with this specific type of expertise; be aware that many agencies, even the global players, have axed their training departments in recent years and may lack this capability. Unless your contract with them is written to your extreme disadvantage, you have the right to select an independent consultant to work hand-in-hand with you and your agency.

- If your issue is liable to incur governmental oversight, prepare your executives who may be called to testify before Congress, state lawmakers, or federal and state regulatory bodies.

- When the attack comes, put that messaging document into action and make it specific to the real-life conditions you now face.
- Insist on periodic reviews of your messaging as the drama unfolds. In some cases – particularly in the early hours of your crisis – this may require hourly or even minute-by-minute adjustments.

Steel Thy Spokespeople

"While terrorist attacks dominate headlines, the threat posed by hacking attacks are the major concern of UK industry," reports *The Telegraph* of London, citing the security consultancy Control Risks ("Hacking is the biggest threat to British business," December 14, 2015). Things are no different elsewhere across the globe.

Without doubt, your enterprise is jeopardized when cybercriminals strike. It is important to realize that company executives and board members are at risk, too. *The Telegraph* article goes on to say that cyberattacks, "could lead to a shake-up of companies' boardrooms."

Elsewhere in the article, Control Risks CEO Richard Fenning claims that, since most companies "tend to be run by older people," they are less capable of understanding the risks. As our British friends might say, "Rubbish!"

While some younger workers might have a solid grasp on the technology, they are generally on shakier ground when it comes to designing and implementing strategy. This is not a knock on youth; it's simply due to the fact that depth of insight comes with time and experience. Should board members invite younger workers with different skills to share their perspectives? Absolutely, and those viewpoints should be factored in to the decision-making process. Decision-making authority, however, needs to rest in experienced hands for swift judgement is often mandated mid-disaster.

Your communications leadership team offers another indispensable viewpoint. You would be wise to earn a seat at the policymaking table before, during, and after any situation, crisis or otherwise.

Your Call to Cyber Action

The next time you read an article about a cyberattack and think, "That could have been us," it's too late. The hackers may have already infiltrated your systems, too. How effectively are you prepared to communicate when that ticking time bomb detonates?

Part of your preparation must involve messaging (see Chapter Eight for a more thorough treatment of messaging). By way of brief review, game out some possible scenarios and run your crisis team through them. Determine:

- What aspects of our message work?
- What doesn't work?
- What surprised us?
- Who shined in the spotlight?
- Who should never speak for us in public settings?

You must take action and prepare before your cybercrisis hits. You will be sorely disappointed if you find yourself scrambling when a crisis jolts you into awareness.

Your leadership must insist – indeed, mandate – that your designated spokespeople be part of a regular communications training regimen. This does not mean that your consultant needs to lead formal workshops every month. What it does mean is that they should design a program that ensures your executives sharpen their communications edge steadily over time.

Yes, the program should involve periodic refresher workshops under your consultant's guidance. Additionally, it should include drills that you can implement internally interspersed with recurrent check-ins.

The health of your business revolves around your ability to respond to a cyberattack. The safety and well-being of your clients, customers, and members is at stake. Your good reputation hangs in the balance.

A cyberattack is bad enough. A failure to communicate when attacked will seal your fate, relegating you and your business to the proverbial "dustbin of history."

Confront Your Crises

I'm a pretty practical guy (as I hope you can tell from this volume), so let's review some down-to-earth steps you can take to gird your business for the crisis lurking around the corner.

Remember that pre-mortem. Before a problem ever hits, gaze over the horizon to assess your strengths and weak spots. Then look for ways to lessen your risk profile. Simply put, you want to avoid trouble, not manage it.

Implement systems that allow you to sniff out danger in real time. Those early warning systems you set up with colleagues in other departments can help you hear early warning bells. Keep your finger on the pulse of a broad range of stakeholders. You never quite know who will raise an alarm or when.

Realize that you will need to fast forward your decision-making process. No, you won't have perfect knowledge as the crisis unfolds. You and your C-suite influencers will have to make some quick choices. Prepare your mindset for that fact and decide as much as you can ahead of time.

Finally, plot out a number of time perspectives. For instance, look beyond quarterly results. Take a medium and longer term look at how your crisis is likely to affect your business and reputation five or 10 years down the road.

Five for the Future

In Chapter Ten you gained some strategies to guide you through your next crisis. How can you best use them when catastrophe strikes? Use these "Five for the Future" discussion questions to help you sustain your C-suite's influence over the long run. Discuss these issues with co-workers, professional colleagues, mentors, and in your own mind:

1. Communicating during a crisis often gets short shrift. What can you do to prepare your firm to communicate with key constituencies during the inevitable crisis?
2. What high-profile disasters most closely paralleled potential dilemmas your business faces? What can you learn from them?
3. Your business is likely to encounter a cybercrisis of some form, if you haven't already. What steps have you taken to prepare?
4. What early warning systems do you have in place to alert you to a catastrophe that may be right around the corner?
5. How do you plan to deal with the public and the media when calamity strikes?

Bonus content

Are you looking for an outline that tells you how to prepare for a crisis? I've got some extra suggestions for you. Log on to www.barkscomm.com/APlusBonus for your free copy of "Nine Crucial Crisis Communications Tips."

RECOMMENDED READING

During my years of research, I've located many resources on communications strategy. Some are quite good. Others lack depth or contain incorrect interpretations.

References recommended here have been created by communications experts who know their stuff. I've sorted through it so you don't have to. I believe these to be the most useful resources.

In assembling this list, I've aimed toward practical resources that business executives will find useful. For that reason, I've mostly avoided academic and technical sources. Online references include links to the relevant documents.

Aula, Pekka and Saku Mantere. *Strategic Reputation Management*. New York: Routledge, 2008.

Barks, Ed. *The Truth About Public Speaking: The Three Keys to Great Presentations* (second edition). Berryville, Virginia: Ogmios Publishing, 2019.

Barnett, Michael L. and Timothy G. Pollock. *The Oxford Handbook of Corporate Reputation*. Oxford, United Kingdom: Oxford University Press, 2012.

Brown, Douglas S. 2012. "After action review: The most eye-opening business success tool," Post University, October 2, accessed July 3, 2018. http://blog.post.edu/2012/10/after-action-review-the-most-eye-opening-business-success-tool.

Cardman, Denise, editor. "All Politics Is Local: A Practical Guide to Effective Advocacy for State and Local Bars." Chicago: American Bar Association, 2016. https://www.americanbar.org/content/dam/aba/publications/GAO/allpoliticsislocal.authcheckdam.pdf

Christiano, Ann, and Annie Neimand. 2017. "The Back-of-the-Envelope Guide to Communications Strategy," *Stanford Social Innovation Review*, September 7, accessed July 10, 2018. https://ssir.org/articles/entry/the_back_of_the_envelope_guide_to_communications_strategy

Cornelissen, Joep P. *Corporate Communications: A Guide to Theory and Practice.* Thousand Oaks, California: Sage Publications, Inc., 2017.

Dezenhall, Eric. *Glass Jaw: A Manifesto for Defending Fragile Reputations in an Age of Instant Scandal.* New York: Twelve, 2014,

Eccles, Robert G., Scott C. Newquist, and Roland Schatz. 2007. "Reputation and Its Risks," *Harvard Business Review*, February, accessed July 3, 2018. https://hbr.org/2007/02/reputation-and-its-risks/ar/1.

Fearn-Banks, Kathleen. *Crisis Communications: A Casebook Approach*, third edition. Mahwah, New Jersey: Lawrence Erlbaum Associates, Inc., 2007.

Fombrun, Charles J. *Reputation: Realizing Value from the Corporate Image.* Boston: Harvard Business School Press, 1996.

Gregory, Anne. *Planning and Managing Public Relations Campaigns: A Strategic Approach.* Philadelphia: Kogan Page, 2010.

Handlin, Amy H. *Be Your Own Lobbyist: How to Give Your Small Business Big Clout with State and Local Government.* Santa Barbara, California: Praeger, 2010.

Haywood, Roger. *Corporate Reputation: The Brand and the Bottom Line.* Sterling, Virginia: Kogan Page US, 2005.

Higgins, Richard B. *The Search for Corporate Strategic Credibility.* Westport, Connecticut: Quorum Books, 1996.

Insurance Journal. 2013. "ACE Study: Reputation the Hardest Risk to Manage," July 23, accessed July 3, 2018. http://www.insurancejournal.com/news/international/2013/07/23/299399.htm.

Lerbinger, Otto. *The Crisis Manager: Facing Disasters, Conflicts, and Failures,* second edition. New York: Routledge, 2011.

Lerbinger, Otto. *Corporate Public Affairs: Interacting with Interest Groups, Media and Government.* New York: Routledge, 2005.

Manhattanville College Institute for Managing Risk, accessed July 3, 2018. https://www.mville.edu/programs/institute-managing-risk.

Marsh/RIMS. 2014. "Organizational Dynamics: A Focus for Effective Risk Management," May, accessed July 3, 2018. https://www.marsh.com/ee/en/insights/research-briefings/excellence-in-risk-management-xii.html

Navarro, Joe. *What Every Body Is Saying.*New York: HarperCollins Publishers, 2008.

Oliver, Sandra. *Public Relations Strategy,* third edition. London: Kogan Page Limited, 2010.

Oliver, Sandra M., editor. *Handbook of Corporate Communication and Public Relations.* New York: Routledge, 2004.

Reputation Institute blog, accessed July 3, 2018. https://blog.reputationinstitute.com.

Ristuccia, Henry. 2014. "Fresh Perspectives on Managing Reputational Risk," *Risk & Compliance Journal,* March 17, accessed July 3, 2018. http://deloitte.wsj.com/riskandcompliance/2014/03/17/fresh-perspectives-on-managing-reputational-risk.

Shapira, Roy. 2014. "Regulation and Reputation," Reputation Institute, accessed July 3, 2018. https://www.reputationinstitute.com/sites/default/files/pdfs/Regulation-and-Reputation-Insights-2015.pdf.

Smith-Bingham, Richard, James Basden, Tracy Knippenburg Gillis, Rick Wise, and Alex Wittenberg. "Reputation Risk - A Rising C-Suite Imperative," accessed July 3, 2018. http://www.oliverwyman.com/our-expertise/insights/2014/may/reputation-risk-a-rising-c-suite-imperative.html.

Van Riel, Cees, and Marijke Baumann. 2015. "Reputation 2020: Ten Trends Driving Reputation Management," Reputation Institute, accessed July 3, 2018. https://www.reputationinstitute.com/research/reputation-2020-ten-trends-driving-reputation-management,

Author's note: My thanks to the staff at the Jefferson Building's Main Reading Room and at the Law Library of the Library of Congress. From the research librarians to the staff who pulls books from the shelves to the cloakroom attendants, we can be grateful for such dedicated, helpful, and pleasant public servants. While I've been using the reading room off and on since my days as a Senate intern decades ago, I never cease to be awed by its grandeur, and humbled to have the opportunity to utilize the world's foremost research facility.

INDEX

ABOUT THE AUTHOR

Communications strategy consultant and author Ed Barks works with communications and government relations executives who counsel their C-suite leaders, and with businesses that need their communications strategy and messaging to deliver bottom line results. They gain an enhanced reputation, greater confidence, more opportunities for career advancement, and achievement of long-term business and public policy goals.

Ed provided his expertise to CBS News when Facebook CEO Mark Zuckerberg prepared to testify before Congress. He is also the author of *The Truth About Public Speaking: The Three Keys to Great Presentations*, and the media relations guide, *Face the Press with Confidence: The Media Interview Companion*.

Ed contributes to a variety of publications and is the former "Speaking Sense" columnist for the *Washington Business Journal*. He has published numerous additional works such as:

- "Eleven Elements to Mold a Magnetic Message: How to Shape Your Story for the Press, Policymakers, and the Public"
- "Beyond the Bottom Line: 20 Ways to Reduce Reputational Risk"
- "Thrill on the Hill: How to Turn Congressional Testimony into Public Policy Success"
- "The Lasting Effects of Media Training: Lifelong Learning or Temporary Phenomenon?"

More than 5,000 business leaders, association executives, scientists, government officials, entertainers, and other thought leaders can thank Ed for sharpening their communications edge.

According to his clients, he "knows how to elicit peak performance." They call him "a master at connecting with his audience" and "an effective educator," and give his communications training workshops "two thumbs up!"

He has served as President of Barks Communications since founding it in 1997. He holds several leadership roles including service on the Board of Governors of the National Press Club and the faculty of the U.S. Chamber of Commerce Institute for Organization Management. He is a former member of the board of directors of the Institute of Management Consultants National Capital Region, and served on the Consultants Section Council of the American Society of Association Executives (ASAE).

An inside-the-Beltway veteran, Ed has spent more than 25 years in Washington, D.C. He brings another critical perspective to his clients' communications needs – that of a broadcaster and journalist. He knows firsthand the tricks and techniques of the reporting trade, thanks to a decade of experience in radio broadcasting.

A Note from Ed Barks

I love to hear from my readers. Here's how you can get in touch:

- On the web at www.barkscomm.com
- Follow my Goodreads author page at www.goodreads.com/EdBarks (while you're there, send me a "Friend" invitation; I will gladly accept)
- Get strategy updates for communications and government relations executives who counsel their C-suite leaders at the C-suite Blueprint blog: https://csuiteblueprint.wordpress.com.
- Join my Communications Community at www.barkscomm.com/communications-community
- Follow me on Twitter at www.twitter.com/EdBarks
- Subscribe to my YouTube channel, MediaTrainingTV, at https://www.youtube.com/MediaTrainingTV
- Email: ebarks@barkscomm.com
- Phone: (540) 955-0600

Thank you for purchasing and reading *A+ Strategies for C-Suite Communications: Turning Today's Leaders into Tomorrow's Influencers.* You could have chosen any number of books to read. I am most grateful and honored that you selected mine.

I hope it helped you propel your C-suite to higher heights, and that it provided tangible benefits to your company's long-range business and public policy goals, and to your career.

You can download all the bonus content contained at the end of each chapter at www.barkscomm.com/APlusBonus.

Now that you've read *A+ Strategies for C-Suite Communications,* I would be most appreciative if you posted a review on Amazon and Goodreads. Whether this book left you inspired, motivated, disappointed, or indifferent, your review is welcome. Your reactions help me update the book periodically, and will prove beneficial in future writing projects. Additionally, your review helps boost the book's popularity.

Please spread the news about *A+ Strategies for C-suite Communications* with your professional colleagues, friends, and family by sharing it on LinkedIn, Twitter, Instagram, Facebook, and your other digital media channels.

Buy the new edition of my first book, *The Truth About Public Speaking: The Three Keys to Great Presentations*, now available in paperback and ebook formats.

Do you want to keep pace with the latest news, including inside information on forthcoming books? Sign up for the monthly Communications Community newsletter at www.barkscomm.com/communications-community.

I enjoy sharing ideas with audiences large and small, for example, your:

- C-suite leadership
- Board of directors
- Communications team
- Government relations team
- Entire staff during employee development day
- Trade association's annual meeting
- Professional society's monthly program
- Book club

To arrange a speaking engagement, call (540) 955-0600.

Made in the USA
Middletown, DE
03 January 2023

21171101R00106